[A Spellbook
   for Male Pagans]

WICCA
SPELLCRAFT
FOR MEN

A.J. Drew

NEW PAGE BOOKS
A division of The Career Press, Inc.
Franklin Lakes, NJ

WICCA SPELLCRAFT FOR MEN
Cover design by Diane Chin
Typeset by Stacey A. Farkas
Printed in the U.S.A. by Book-mart Press

To order this title, please call toll-free 1-800-CAREER-1 (NJ and Canada: 201-848-0310) to order using VISA or MasterCard, or for fur-ther information on books from Career Press.

The Career Press, Inc., 3 Tice Road, PO Box 687, Franklin Lakes, NJ 07417

www.careerpress.com
www.newpagebooks.com

Library of Congress Cataloging-in-Publication Data

Drew, A. J.
    Wicca spellcraft for men : a spellbook for male pagans / by A. J. Drew
        p. cm.
    Includes bibliographical references and index.
    ISBN 1-56414-495-X
    1. Witchcraft. I. Title.

BF1571.5.M45 D743 2001
133.4'4—dc21   00-066451

Dedication

For Brandon Teena (1972–1993)
because you were twice the man that I can aspire to be.

Acknowledgments

Any human accomplishment is the result of every moment previous to that accomplishment. The completion of a book is no exception. It is only when we narrow the field that we can place names on the individual contributors to any one project. With that accomplished, when one of the names that remains has had no direct involvement with the particular project, it becomes obvious that that person was one of the most tremendous influences in the author's life.

My mother, Ann, has gone far beyond being a tremendous influence. She has been empowering and supportive in every way a son could dream. Without her love and guidance, I could not have learned how to type, much less author a book. Although at times I might refer to him as a character rather than an influence, my brother Stephen must also be acknowledged for his support and willingness to explore some of my more ridiculous ideas. Great thanks to my father for encouraging me to join the U.S. military and tremendous thanks to the U.S. Army for showing me how to be an adult. My father was a loving but stern man. It took a lot to impress him. If he were alive today, I am sure he would have been proud to see my first book in print. Fortunately, my military service gave him what he needed to be proud of me before he died. Also to be thanked as family are Steven Sowers for being my closest of friends, and Susan Sowers for not killing him, even when he asked her to.

Special thanks to Todd "The Hat" Rinehart, Tatia Kingslady, Robert "Osyr" Clark, Rebecca "Celene" King, Linda "Sky" Fainey, and Ruth "Bunny" Merrill: Todd and Tatia for the loan of rare books that were necessary for research; Rebecca and Robert for affording me the time to take a more active role in the Real Witches Ball 2000, which led to many inclusions in this book; and Linda for keeping the customers happy but at bay when I was writing in the back room of my store. I also thank my lawyer and friend Ruth for letting me know just how far an author can go without risking a lawsuit.

Every author who has acknowledged an editor has been accused of pandering the sale of a second book. This being the second of my books that Mike Lewis has worked with, I will risk the accusations. I live a very simple life, earning most of my income from clay works. I rarely wear shoes, and the one tie that I own has a Harley Davidson Springer front end on it. As you can imagine, I am not what readers envision when they think of an author. With that said, I offer many thanks to Mike Lewis for putting up with this big Yeti and helping me clarify and organize my thoughts.

I thank Patricia Telesco for pointing me in the right direction, Sirona Knight for keeping me on track, and Dorothy Morrison for offering the icon of brass to which every man should aspire. These three women are the finest people a human can ever meet. I would not have considered writing my first book without "Mama Trish's" nudging, and I would not have stuck with my own voice if not for the reassurance of both Sirona and Dorothy that many others see things as I do.

Before Mike, Patricia, Sirona, and Dorothy came into my life, there was a woman who unknowingly gave birth to what has become my greatest resource of ideas. Great thanks to Leslie "the Frog Lady" Mehne; I will love you forever. Thank you for all of your encouragement during the time we spent together and thank you for the suggestion that I create the Web site that has become the most significant influence on my writing.

Finally, thanks to each of the thousands upon thousands of community members at *www.neopagan.com*. Collectively, you have given me an unprecedented access to a pagan community that is unrestrained by age, race, sex, income, and even geographic location. It is from the members at *www.neopagan.com* that I drew the confidence needed to write to an audience of my peers in a voice of my own. To each and every member, "Blessed be and live free!"

Contents

spiritual choice, we now stand faced with the very real fact that we are becoming an issue of amusement.

Nowhere is this problem more prevalent than in the area of spellcraft. It seems there is a new book on spellcraft every day. Again and again, we are expected to believe that a red candle will bring you love and a special chant will put you knee deep in cash. These books are insulting to everyone except for the most gullible. It wasn't long ago that John Q. Public thought Witches killed babies and drank their virgin blood. Today, Mr. and Mrs. Public think we are crazy. Take the word of a man who has worked in the Wiccan community for many years: the Publics are very often right. There are many Wiccans that just haven't figured out that our religion is not a role-playing game.

I do look like the Hermet Druid card in the stronghold expansion set of Magick the Gathering, but I do not claim to be a powerful magician. In like fashion, I also do not claim to be a 32nd-level wizard in the latest incarnation of Dungeons and Dragons or any other form of recreation. To be perfectly honest, I have trouble setting the timer on my VCR. I don't wear a lot of black clothes, spikes, or black fingernail polish. All things taken into consideration, I am rather boring. I wouldn't even stand out in a crowd if not for the tremendous amount of hair on my head and face that I have no hope of ever controlling.

I am a simple Wiccan with a simple goal: to live my life to its fullest potential. I don't summon demons to do my bidding, nor do I blow flames from my fingertips, so I am not going to deceive you. Life is not always what we expect, desire, or deserve and you can't change that by waving a magick wand. What you can change is how you react and interact with what you encounter.

In my efforts to achieve that goal, I have had the fortune of becoming many things. I have been a son, husband, soldier, poet, sculptor, silversmith, computer programmer, shopkeeper, and very recently, an author (although after the publication of this book, that last title might be forcibly removed). But even with spellcraft, my life has not been anywhere near perfect. I have also been unemployed, divorced, homeless, and hungry. Life has not always been joyful, and I have not found those special magick words that solve each of life's challenges. Even with magick, I have been unable to help the ones that I love. I sat with my father and watched the final hours of his life slip away as cancer won its final battle against his body.

Many will find the words of this book entirely too harsh for their tender ears. Hear them nonetheless. If they damage your sensibilities, then heal yourself in the arms of our great lady and her earthly representatives. But if you are not willing to allow even your sensibilities to become damaged, then you have no right nor reason to litter her arms.

My words are sometimes harsh because they come from the real world that is sometimes harsh. So if you picked up this book because you wanted relief from that real world, you should put it down this very moment. Magick is a very real part of the real world! Magick is life and magick is death, but most of all magick is the way we cope with both.

Magick and Spellcraft in Theory

I have incorporated the use of magick in my everyday life for many years. For the first few years, I did so without ever questioning why certain practices worked. I simply purchased the typical spellbooks and did what the author said would work. Sometimes the spells seemed to work and sometimes they seemed not to. After a couple years of trying every spell that claimed to offer the results I desired, I found myself wondering why some worked and some did not. To answer that question, I had to determine how spells worked.

Finding books to aid my discovery was difficult. The only thing spellbooks had to offer was what supposedly worked for the author or what reportedly worked in the Middle Ages. Then I stumbled onto a book called *Magick in Theory and Practice* by

Aleister Crowley. The book contains a very sound theory on how magick works. However, the book has very little to do with spells and almost nothing to do with spellcraft in a Wiccan context. Upon reading the book, I realized why my search had been so fruitless. There is a very clear difference between magick and spellcraft. It is the difference between how all internal combustion engines work and how a particular motorcycle works.

Section I is not only my explanation of how the internal combustion engine (magick) works, but how one particular motorcycle works. In this case, the motorcycle is a beautiful Harley Davidson called Wiccan spellcraft. More importantly, this is my theory on how the two interact with each other and how spellcraft creates a greater chance of magick taking place.

don't let it fool you. We are not safe from our own minds. Because manifestations don't tend to be as dramatic as sword and sorcery movies, we have virtually ignored the daily manifestations that do happen. A lack of skill does not mean the untrained mind is unable to cause large manifestations and changes. It just means the manifestations will not be guided by clear intent. Changing the tiniest of things can cause great changes in our lives. The difference between a perfectly healthy mind and suicidal depression is only a tiny change in brain chemistry.

A great portion of this mastery is simply learning what our true intent is. Instead of running haphazardly through our lives, accepting the state of being that our every whim deals, we can determine what it is that we intend to accomplish and then determine the best method to achieve that intent while avoiding the daily whims that seek to distract us.

Even the slightest whim can certainly cause difficulty in our lives. Mentally healthy people do not deliberately sabotage their own lives, but causing undesired manifestations is as easy as self-doubt. Reverse the visualization conducted by the Zen archer. What would happen if he visualized the arrow missing the target?

If we can cause health through a positive mental image, surely we can cause illness with a negative mental image. Referring back to the placebo example, if we take a sugar pill thinking it will make us well, we tend to become well. What if we take the same sugar pill thinking it will make us sick? We have the ability to manifest both creative and destructive influences on our health. Medical science has accepted this as fact for many years. The phenomenon is commonly called psychosomatic illness.

Remember those studies on prayer. If keeping another person's health in our mind will cause their health to improve, what happens when we keep a person's illness in our mind? If a parent constantly worries about his child becoming ill, chances are his child will become ill.

Once the manifestation has taken place, it is difficult to end. When we perceive an illness with our senses, those perceptions become a mental image. Because the thought of a sick person will tend to manifest a sick person, we can see another important magickal guideline taking shape.

Magickal Guideline: Like attracts like

Most men have experienced the "taken man" syndrome. When you are not in a relationship, women don't seem interested in you. But when you are in a relationship, women start to notice you. When that relationship becomes serious, women really start to notice you. The more committed the relationship becomes, the more women seem to want you. If only we had a cosmic hold button.

There are no coincidences, but there are patterns. You attract more women who want a relationship with you when you have the clear image of a relationship with a woman. Being in a relationship automatically generates that clear mental image. The mind works in both directions. What you see inside the mind tends to manifest outside the mind. What you see outside the mind tends to manifest inside the mind. If there is a woman in your life, your mind will tend to manifest women in your life. If you are surrounded by poverty, you will tend to manifest poverty. Your mind acts on all that you perceive. The more you consider a situation, the more attached you become to that situation.

If it were only that simple, you could think of something and it would happen. But controlling the mind is not nearly that simple. Try thinking about anything for more than a moment or two. Try concentrating on one thing and absolutely nothing else. How long until you have to scratch or cough? How long until the position you are sitting in becomes painful?

A good way to gauge and improve your ability to concentrate is to close your eyes and visualize a cube floating in a sea of nothing. Concentrate on that cube and nothing else. Assign a color to each face of the cube. Concentrate on that one object for as long as you can without thinking of anything else. In your mind, rotate the cube horizontally and then vertically. Can you

5. *Test* that hypothesis. If the test confirms your hypothesis, conduct it again to make sure.

6. Draw a *conclusion* based on the experiment as to whether or not your hypothesis was correct. If correct, record your conclusion and all matters that may have contributed to it. If your hypothesis was not correct, go back to Step 3.

At this point, you might be wondering if I have an obsession with deodorant and toothpaste. Yes, I do. Actually, my issue is with common sense. No matter how many candles you burn, your love life will be dismal if you do not bathe. No matter how many chants you recite, you probably won't get a job if you don't look for one. When searching for explanations, do not try to separate the magickal from the mundane. There is no separation between magick and the real world because magick is a function of the real world. Remember that the principles of science and magick are the same. In each, the simplest explanation is most often the most correct explanation. Science expresses this principle as *Ockham's razor.*

♦ ♦ ♦

Ock·ham's razor also **Oc·cam's razor** (kmz rzr) *n.* A rule in science and philosophy stating that entities should not be multiplied needlessly. This rule is interpreted to mean that the simplest of two or more competing theories is preferable and that an explanation for unknown phenomena should first be attempted in terms of what is already known. Also called **law of parsimony.**

(From *The American Heritage Dictionary of the English Language, Third Edition*)

♦ ♦ ♦

Like science, magick has generally accepted principles. You don't have to put your hand in fire to know that it will burn. Someone has already done it and his findings are recorded. Science likes to call these explanations *laws.* It wasn't long ago that scientific law said the flow of electricity was exactly opposite of how scientific law says it flows today. The former law of electricity is now known as the common theory of electricity.

In magickal terms, these generally accepted principles are called *models*. When these models are used to explain deity, they are called *archetypes*. When they are used to explain magickal properties, they are called *lore*.

Lore tells us that using a broom to sweep the temple area before ritual begins will cleanse the area of negative energies. A very small number of Wiccans probably think the broom is literally throwing the negative energy from the circle. Most do it because it is part of their tradition (another word for lore) but have absolutely no idea why it works.

To become proficient at spellcraft, you must recognize the sweeping as a model that assists our visualization of clearing the circle. We see the broom moving back and forth. We hear it sweeping across the ground. We feel the broom within our hands and feel our muscles move in the familiar pattern of sweeping away the things that we do not want in our home. The physical act of sweeping is a method of triggering your mind to clear the circle. In group ritual, even when you do not instruct the visualization, a collective effect is achieved because everyone is familiar with the model. Everyone has used a broom. Because everyone sees the action, everyone's mind has been sent the signal that we are sweeping out what we do not want in the circle. With that thought implanted in their minds, everyone will attempt to manifest a cleaned circle even if they do not know it is what they are doing.

Your senses carry messages directly to your mind. Anything that you see, hear, taste, smell, and feel will affect your mind. It is not a coincidence that fast-food restaurants have hard seats and yellow decorations. The hard seat feels fine for about 30 minutes. After that, it then becomes distractingly uncomfortable. This is approximately the same amount of time it takes the yellow to cause similar distraction. At first, the color stimulates your hunger but after about a half an hour yellow tends to upset the stomach. The intent of the restaurant management is for you to come, eat, and leave relatively quickly so they have seats for the next customer. To that end, they determined the conditions that would improve their odds of causing the desired behavior in customers. Have you ever noticed that even though the popcorn machine is running, movie theaters tend to stock the machine with previously popped corn? The popcorn is made when it is practical. The machine runs to generate the scent of popcorn to entice moviegoers. If commercial establishments can use your senses to manipulate your mind for their benefit, surely you can do it for your benefit. After all, whose mind it?

Each of our senses has the ability to either work with us or against us. Each can help to establish conditions favorable to either success or failure. Once we are aware of the many things that enter our mind, we can better manipulate conditions to be favorable for success.

Sight

Vision is the sense that we rely on the most. This explains why it is also the sense so many spells focus on. Tell someone you are casting a spell, and they will inevitably think candles will be involved. The flame makes a great focal point for meditation.

Ceiling paint usually contains a hint of blue so slight that it cannot be consciously perceived. But the almost invisible hint of blue makes a room feel more relaxed, the way a home should. Lore tells us that the seven primary colors have been associated with different functions of the mind. Blue is associated with calming influences. Chakra lore teaches that blue stimulates peace, truth, and quiet order.

No occult store would be complete without the New Orleans-style voodoo doll. But it isn't the driving of a pin into the doll that causes change; it is your vision of the pin driving into the person that the doll represents that causes change. The doll is just a prop to help you visualize. The same is the case when a human image is used for healing. Human-shaped candles are often burned to aid in health. As the flame burns through the candle, the visualization is to view the sickness burning away from the body. Sometimes the visualization involves seeing a white light of health enter the body. Whichever works the best for you is the one you should use.

Protect your mind from visual assaults. Everything that you see has already entered your mind and will try to manifest. If you want some sense of order in your life, you should force yourself to establish a sense of order in your home. Wash your dishes, do your laundry, and make your bed on a regular basis (okay, maybe you don't have to make your bed). If you wake every morning to see an unkept house, your mind will manifest the condition. The condition of your home may well be a leading factor in the inability to successfully complete a job interview. Your potential employer does not see your kitchen, but you do.

Smell

The sense of smell functions twice as fast as your sense of touch. Of all the senses, it connects the strongest to our memory. The smell of salt might trigger memories of the ocean. The smell of freshly mowed hay might remind us of Spring. It is possible that the scent of new mown hay could trigger Springtime mating habits. Scent cannot completely control behavior, but it can certainly nudge or push us in deliberate directions. Pheromones in fresh sweat can promote sexual passion. Have you ever noticed how mosquitoes never bite some people while other people are almost literally eaten alive by the insects? Those same pheromones are what drive away insects. If scent can turn women on and turn mosquitoes off, you can imagine the range of other capabilities.

Aromatherapy has reached almost fad popularity because the basics work without any level of skill or awareness. It is as easy as putting a few drops of essential oil of lavender on a diffuser to get a good night's sleep. Individual scents each promote different responses.

Mixtures can be used to achieve more advanced goals. But you will not be able to create or customize those mixtures without the knowledge of how the blend works. Money-drawing oil does not have the power to run out, grab the lucky lottery numbers,

Robes dramatically decrease the amount of distraction that normal clothes cause while providing security of knowing we are not breaking social taboo. When you wear nothing but a robe, you never have to worry about your shirt coming untucked, your belt that is too tight, your zipper being open, or hiking your britches because your waist is larger than your hips. If you wear undergarments, you are completely defeating the purpose of the robe, as undergarments are typically the most restricting and distracting part of our outfit. If that idea alarms you, remember that we are always naked under our clothes. If that does not help, seek qualified professional counseling.

If you are practicing in a public place or if you must be seen in public on your way to or from a rite, the robe itself will probably be a distraction. Rather than distracting yourself by challenging social convention, find other ways to protect your mind from tactile assaults. Get rid of those tight-fitting jeans. Buy a pair of suspenders and loosen your belt. Purchase a bed that doesn't leave your back full of kinks and wash the bedding that causes you to itch.

Hearing

Everything that we hear will affect the mind. In order to understand what we are told, our mind must process the sound and turn it into meaning. Even when words are not spoken out loud, the mind processes the information contained in those words in the same way. The only difference between the thought of a word and the spoken word is that the spoken word is generally easier to exchange.

A child can only hear how worthless he is so many times before the child starts believing it himself. Sometimes the easiest way to prevent verbal assaults is to simply get away from the people who cause the harm. Failing that, we can establish empowerments that reinforce our defenses against such attacks. When I was really in need of verbal empowerment, I almost had the words *you have value* tattooed on my wrist so I would be reminded to say the words daily.

Hearing is particularly effective when it is the spoken word that is being heard. Language is much more direct than symbolism. Generally speaking, words have set meanings. The down side to language is that, because it is so direct, it is easy to unknowingly use this sense to your own detriment. If you are receiving words of encouragement from your friends and peers, do not argue with them.

If we say something over and over, we will begin to believe it. In ritual, I always conduct the outsider offering. In so doing, I verbally affirm that I want to rid myself of attributes that I consider undesirable: "These are the ones that challenged the gods and lost! These are greed, bigotry, and ignorance. There is no place in our circles or in our minds for these creatures."

The outsiders are then symbolically taken outside of the circle. Hearing those words causes others to affirm that we wish to rid ourselves of those attributes. As our personal vision of god is that which we aspire to resemble, identifying things that we do not aspire to with those who challenged the gods provides positive reinforcement of self-image. If we hear the words enough times, we will believe and manifest that belief. Hardly anyone actively listens to the content of radio commercials, but we do tend to remember the brand names. Later, we manifest those brand names in our lives by purchasing the products.

Verse and repetition are the most effective ways to use the sense of hearing to focus the mind. If you were to run as far as you could, how far would you get? If I gave you a set of magick words to recite over and over again, do you think you could double that distance?

> "To bind ye spell every time, let ye spell be spake in rhyme"
> —*the poem of the Wiccan Rede*

The military certainly believes that it works. Drill sergeants might not know exactly what they are doing when they call cadence, but it still works. The process of hearing and repeating

The horned one is protector and God of death

Cernunnos (Celtic)—God in charge of the underworld and death. Under another potential name (Hu Gadarn), he once protected the Earth by ending the great flood. When we recognize his wife as Mother Earth, the protection theme is clear.

Faunus (Roman)—His wife is Fauna, goddess of the fields. Their marriage illustrates the protection aspect of men and their women. He is the protector of the fields and his wife is a personification of the fields. With his name Lupercus, his festival Lupercalia is celebrated on February 15. Traditionally this is done in Lupercal, a cave at the bottom of the Palatin hill. This is the same cave where Romulus and Remus were reared by a wolf.

Faunus/Lupercus reminds us that contrary to popular fiction, blood sacrifice was made to pagan gods. Each year, two goats and a dog were sacrificed at Lupercal. The goats were sacrificed in thanks for his aid in protecting the shepherds' goats from the wolf and the dog because it was the protector of the flock. Although I would never advise the sacrifice of animals specifically for religious purposes, there is historic precedent. As such, I can see how blood rites could be worked into the normal killing and consumption of animals that is condoned by our society. In other words, bless your meat and remember that even though it was probably purchased in the grocery store, the exact same amount of death was involved as if you sacrificed it on an altar.

Hermes (Greek)—He is directly associated with death and the guide of souls to the world beyond this lifetime. He is sometimes considered a trickster and the god of thieves. His Roman god form is Mercury, but in that form he traded his horns for a winged hat named petasus. Although it is often said that the only horned god of the Celts was Cernunnos, the worship of Mercury was included in Celtic lore as their Gaulish Mercury. Wiccans are rarely told that Mercury was also known as Alipes and identified as Woden, who is the Anglo-Saxon form of Odin (Scandinavian). Could this oversight have taken place due to his other attributes? Woden later became the warrior's god and as such he is associated with war and death. Odin's other associations to the horned god include his love of poetry (as in Hermes) and his ability to drive men insane (as in Pan). It is also interesting to note that Odin is usually accompanied by Freki and Geri, two wolves to whom Odin gives all his food (sacrifice) as he consumes nothing but wine. When the final battle comes at Ragnarok, the Fenris Wolf will consume Odin. One can easily see the similarities with the sacrifice made to Faunus/Lupercus to keep the wolves away.

Surely no greater connection can be made between Odin and the horned gods than that of sacrifice. Pierced by his own spear, Odin hung on the world tree for nine days. From this sacrifice, he received the runes (written language). Additionally, he has only one eye, as he traded the other for a single drink from the well of knowledge.

Herne (British)—The hunter who causes death so that there can be life. He is often pictured with a huge erect phallus. He is strongly associated with the wild hunt that was much like the wild hunt of Dionysus/Bacchus. Interesting to note that Dionysus is sometimes described as having hair that is curled up like horns. See notes on Priapus for more connections to Dionysus.

Pan (Greek)—Of Pan, the Farrars say "If you mess him about—beware. He can be a very chaotic god." Pan has been brought to great anger. He once had a nymph torn to pieces for refusing his affections. Pan struck such fear into the hearts of men that his very name is itself the root of the word *panic*. He was called on during the Battle of Marathon, where he so terrified the Persians that they left the conflict screaming in near madness. The descendants of the victors would worship him for generations afterwards, but not because he was a kind and gentle god. They worshipped him because he ruthlessly attacked the minds of their enemies and drove them off.

Priapus (Greek)—Carvings made of fig wood were made to invoke his favors. These carvings featured a huge erect phallus much the way Herne was depicted. You will recall the connection between Herne and Dionysus/Bacchus in the wild hunt. Here we see another connection, in the Greek, Priapus as the son of Dionysus.

The archetypes are needed in their totality because they accurately reflect the totality of the human condition. If you simply deny your own rage, you will not be able to effectively control it. What could be your ally will become your enemy. Consider the man who denies his own lust. His intent may be to remain in a monogamous relationship but he will fail if he perpetuates the lie that another woman could turn his eye.

Intent is a function of the mind; what affects our minds will affect our intent. This is one of the many reasons there is a difference between what will be magickally effective for men and women. Simply put, the male mind is physically designed to think about mating much more often than the female mind.

Do not confuse mating practices with sexual intercourse. Although sex can definitely be a part of our mating habits, it is a very small part. We spend much more time trying to find, protect, and provide for our mates than we do having sex with them. Women might not want to hear this, but this physical difference contributes greatly to the situation in which men are generally on top in the workplace, in sports, and in any other situation where competitiveness is a virtue. Some women like to claim this is due to the "glass ceiling," an invisible barrier that the male conspirators have constructed above women's current position so they cannot elevate themselves.

◆ ◆ ◆

Ockham's razor—It is more likely that men will succeed in an area where masculine traits are valued.

◆ ◆ ◆

Men are generally more successful in competitive activities because men are generally driven to be more competitive. Our mating instinct drives us the same way it drives the males of almost every other species on Earth. It drives us to be competitive, aggressive, forceful, and projective for the purpose of securing and then providing for the best possible mate. No matter where you go, you will still be who you are. I doubt things are very different between Wall Street and the woods of upstate New York. Men are generally more apt to be promoted because not only are we willing, we are driven to rut and butt horns. In a system that values such drive, we are more valued.

Recently, "herstory" has tried to replace history with the claim that before Christianity, the world was operated as a matriarchy. Supporters of herstory claim that women were in charge and the creator was viewed as female. As evidence of this, the Venus of Willendorf is often cited as being as old as 27,000 B.C.E. Chances are, the creator was envisioned as female before humanity discovered the link between sex and pregnancy. Common sense tells us that link would have been discovered the moment "Al Bundy" Caveman noticed that ugly cave women did not get pregnant.

There is absolutely no evidence that the Venus of Willendorf was a veneration of the divine female, much less that it proves women ran the world at the time of its creation. The find is prehistoric. As such, there are no written records of the sculptor's intent. For all we know, it was made to insult the wife of another clan member.

I do believe it was a veneration of the reproductive properties of women because it does seem to be common sense. I do not believe it is proof that at the time women ruled the world, because that does not make sense. I have sculpted a few thousand things. Recently, I sculpted a figure of a ferret. If you saw the way I treat my ferret you might think I worship her, but I assure you that ferrets are the only ones who think that ferrets rule the world.

If women ruled anything in a time where the most effective weapon was roughly equivalent to a pointy stick, men would have knocked them down and taken what they ruled. I draw this conclusion because this is exactly what men have attempted to do to every other "ruler."

Men and women have not had a ruler versus slave relationship except where that relationship was dictated outside of the normal relations of a man and woman. When it comes to magickal practices, that relationship has been greatly influenced by the Christian church a la Medieval Europe.

The Church state was male dominated, but it was not functioning in the best interest of either men or women. The Church state functioned in the best interest of the Church state. It is easy to see how women would get the short end of the stick in a society that is ruled by a male-dominated power structure. However, the great majority of that time period's men were not officials of the Church. The actions of the Church were tremendously disempowering of men as well.

The Christian religion is mostly based on pre-Christian customs and practices. This can be seen in the correspondences between the holy days as well as the Catholic saints and pagan deities. It can also be seen in a number of pagan philosophers that are quoted and paraphrased in the Christian bible. Take out everything that is pagan from Christianity and you are left with virtually nothing. Why then was the Church created? To do exactly what it almost achieved, to rule the face of the earth. As a result, the incorporation of pagan teachings was twisted for that purpose.

It would be irresponsible if I did not point out that the power structure that I am referring to no longer exists. It is just as ridiculous to blame today's Christians for the actions of the Church state of the Middle Ages as it is to blame today's men for the actions of the men of the same time period. It would be inaccurate if I did not also mention that there were patriarchal cultures that pre-date Christianity. But I do not believe the rediscovery of Western magickal practices has been as greatly influenced by any other single historical entity. As most of us live in the aftermath of the Church state, it is necessary to understand what it did in order to overcome its current influence.

Before the Church state, magick and religion were not the separate things that the Church would later insist they were. In the transition of what was magick into what would become Christian doctrine, a great deal was changed. Guidelines became laws and distraction became sin. Where magickal guidelines said women were a tremendous source of potential distraction, Christianity taught the law that woman were the source of the greatest sin. The ultimate manifestation of this trend can be seen in the

belief that women were responsible for original sin. Eve reportedly earned women that title by distracting Adam from his intent
to obey his god.

From a magickal viewpoint, it is not the apple that is the
problem. It is your desire of the apple that causes the problem.
Magickally speaking, there are a few ways you can approach the
apple dilemma. You can abstain from apples, hoping your craving will diminish. You can find the part of your body that causes
the craving and lob it off. Or you can make sure you have plenty
of apples. As you can guess, my choice is the latter.

Abstinence

To avoid distraction (sin), the Church insisted men should
abstain from sexual intercourse. Most often, this instruction even
included their wives. There should be no joy in sex; after all, that
might be distracting. Sex was for procreation and procreation
only. In the case of clergy, indulgence of any kind was forbidden
even when it was for the purpose of procreation. Yes, it flew in
the face of the whole 'be fruitful and multiply' instruction from
their god, but the Church couldn't let women have an influence
on their male leaders. They had to stay the course and win that
big game.

Castration

As an extreme measure of devotion, members of some sects
have even used castration as a mode of enlightenment. I am thinking a little foreskin might be an acceptable thing to give up for
one's religion, but my testicles will be staying exactly where they
are, thank you. These sects are not generally heard of because, as
you can imagine, there were not a lot of members.

Indulgence

Then there is the third option, but the Church ignored this
one. If you are horny, have sex. Doesn't it seem like a rather simple
equation? Appearances can be very deceptive. When was the last

time you had "simple sex"? For the most part, that portion of your brain simply does not stop at conquest. As I said previously, the mating drive is a great deal more than simply having sex. Before you know it, you find yourself in a committed relationship and you became all but useless to the Church state. How could they take over the world if their priests had to pick up their kids after football practice? What they were really saying was that you shouldn't enjoy sex because your brain might kick in and tell you that your potential wife and family is important. It is much easier to rule when your subjects do not use their minds.

The Church knew how strong the mating drive was in men. That knowledge was well established in our archetypes long before Christianity. If they were going to rule the world, they had to raise an army. The mating instinct would drive men to protect their own, but the Church had something entirely different in mind.

Without the intervention of a third party, women tend to become the center of men's lives. If the Church could secure that position for their god, it could solicit men to protect their god. As the Church was the earthly representative of god, it would be what men would die and kill for. To that end and not for the purpose of securing a heavenly place for your immortal soul, the first option was put into place. The head of every man became god and the head of every woman became man. Instead of the natural relationship of give and take that once developed between men and women, we were set on a path of owner and slave. What they failed to mention was that the Church would own every master.

For the most part, the brainwashing worked. The Church state taught that their god was more important than your wife or family. At every turn, the church rebuked the natural mating drive. Eventually, that drive was beaten so far down into our primal identity that it might as well have been missing entirely from our psyche. Even when it slipped from its cage during our dreams, the Church taught that it was the treachery of women. So much did men believe the teachings of the Church, that a wet dream or a morning erection often resulted in the death of the woman the man had dreamt about.

During the burning times, women were easy prey because they were no longer sacred to their men. The protector and provider was no longer a role that men played for their family. Before Christianity, women were an equal part of creation. After Christianity, they were the source of original sin. Some claim that as many as nine million European women were put to death on a charge of witchcraft. Although this figure is probably inflated, can you imagine what would have happened if nine million European men had objected?

Nine million European husbands didn't object because the Church had spiritually castrated them. How inclined would you be to fight with your genitals cut off? Therein lies the reason our spellcraft is not as effective as it once was. We have been spiritually castrated.

Wicca does not see sin where we find distraction. Wiccan spellcraft is different from many Western teachings of magick in that it does not teach that abstinence of the senses will lead to better concentration. We know we cannot turn off our senses, so Wiccans use them to assist us in our goals. Instead of taking an oath of silence (abstaining from hearing our own words), Wiccans make it a point of speaking positive affirmations. Instead of fasting (abstaining from taste), Wiccans make it a point to consume foods that correspond to our intent. Instead of preventing the senses from receiving input that might distract, Wiccans use those senses to reinforce our intent. When it comes to men, instead of ignoring our predisposition towards mating practices, we can use that drive to better develop the manifestations of our intent.

Wicca offers the great promise of restoring the balance of the pre-Christian fertility religions. But balance and equality are not synonyms. Apples and oranges can be equal in weight and they can be equal in volume, but they cannot be equal. Men and women can be equal under the law. We can have equal rights, but we are not equal.

are grouped together and presented as a set of religious values, they become religious morals.

Hindu teachings call it the yama. Buddhism calls it the sila. Judaism calls it the Law of Moses. Christianity call it the "Sermon on the Mount" and Wicca calls it the Rede. Each is a collection of social ethics and guidelines that partially define the religion to which it belongs.

You should not try following these ethics just because they are part of your religion. Instead, they should be a part of your religion because you follow them. Your choice of religion should be a carefully considered decision, which allows an environment in which your personal ethics can exist harmoniously with your religious morals. If you have chosen your religion well, that religious group's sense of morality will also be your ethics. If not, then you will likely run into some rather unsettling problems.

If the morals of your religion are compatible with your personal ethics, then they are much more than a set of rules. They are your magickal warnings. They warn you when you are getting too close to an issue that will distract the mind from your intent. Unlike speed limits and stop signs, there is always a witness present when you break one of your own rules. You are that witness, you are the judge, and in very extreme situations you are the executioner.

Consider the life of a gay man within a religion that teaches homosexuality is an abomination against the Creator. By accepting that religion's sense of morality, he accepts a set of ethics that cause his intent to be in conflict. On one hand, he wants to be in a loving relationship with someone that he finds sexually desirable. On the other hand, he wants to live a moral life. As you can imagine, short of rejecting the morals of that religion, he will not be able to achieve any level of happiness.

This is one of the greatest reasons for the recent swell of the Wiccan community. The one ethic that our community seems to teach contains only eight words, "An ye harm none do what ye will." You can see how such a liberal ethic would appeal to a wider range of people. But the simplicity of this ethic is deceptive. One of the reasons the man in the previous paragraph found his intent in conflict was because he wanted to like himself. He wanted to believe he was moral.

With the possible exception of sociopaths, we all want to feel that way. A simplistic interpretation of the Wiccan Rede does not allow this feeling unless one is content to go through life without incident, challenge, or accomplishment.

If Wicca is truly a nature-based religion, the Wiccan Rede could not possibly instruct that we may not cause harm. Consider natural law. If a fox catches a rabbit for his dinner, is the fox living in compliance with the Wiccan Rede? After all, he did harm the rabbit. The answer is simple: The Wiccan Rede does not instruct that we may not cause harm. It simply instructs that if no harm is taking place, then there is no reason that we should not do as we will. And what happens when our will does cause harm?

This was probably the question that was on Doreen Valiente's mind when she wrote the Poem of the Wiccan Rede. Within her poem, we find further instructions that include both "live and let to live" as well as "fairly take and fairly give." Without examination, these two statements do not appear to be able to exist harmoniously in the fox and rabbit situation. Examination is the key. To do so is a function of the mind. This is exactly what Wiccan morality calls on us to do.

No one can be completely sure where the Wiccan Rede came from, but we do have enough clues to make a very educated guess. Aleister Crowley wrote, "Do what thou wilt shall be the whole of the law." As Crowley and Gerald Gardner were colleagues, it doesn't seem like much of a leap to say that the origins of the Wiccan Rede can be found in Crowley's Law of Thelema. By disassociating the Rede from its most likely origin, we also disassociate the principles that were once associated with its creation. Crowley believed that if one followed his own will, it would be very unlikely that there would be conflicts with the will of others. If, and only if, the rare occasion that the will of two men were in conflict, resolution should be found in fighting as brothers.

Because I am a vegetarian, the Rede instructs me not to eat meat. But because I interpret the Rede only for myself, I have no problem eating tofu delight at the same table as a friend who is eating a hamburger. However, if anyone should ever try to force me to eat meat, I assure you I will fight like a brother to prevent the occurrence. Because my natural mother placed me in an adoption service that found me a wonderful home, I also interpret the Rede as instructing that abortions are wrong. But because I interpret the Rede only for myself, I tend to vote pro-choice.

Many of the ethical decisions that we are faced with come with a tremendous emotional toll. So much is this the case that it is typically difficult for us to predict ahead of time what our responses to any given situation will be. What happens should I find myself the father of an unborn child whose mother intends an abortion? I hope to never find myself in that situation, but if I do, I trust that my ethics will pull me through.

Religious morals can be a hindrance or strength in any effort, but because spellcraft and magick are so deeply dependent on the functions of the mind, how you think about a particular magickal aspiration will greatly affect its outcome. Thus, in order to afford the highest chances for success, every Wiccan spell must be cast in accordance with the ethics of the person who is casting the spell.

If you have practiced Wicca for any length of time, you have probably had a few stray ethics thrown at you time and time again. A couple of these ethics have become so popular that some might consider them part of the Wiccan sense of morality. I do not. Wicca is a religion of the individual. As such, the individual must decide what is and is not a Wiccan moral and in so doing, the decision is only made for that individual.

Popular false moral: You should never attempt manipulative magick

All acts of magick are acts of manipulation. Consider what you have previously heard or read about "manipulative magick" elsewhere. Most Wiccan literature claims that manipulative magick is bad. Our social ethics tend to agree, but only to a point.

It is typically illegal to use subliminal messages to increase sales, but it is legal to use the same delivery method to prevent shoplifting. Far be it for me (a shop owner) to encourage shoplifting, but I have to wonder who decided this makes sense. As theft is an issue of ethics and shopping is an issue of commerce, I wonder who decided it was okay to bombard our senses with someone else's code of ethics. The very people who are trying to instill ethics are conducting themselves in a manner that many would consider unethical. What's next, subliminal messages that tell us to be fruitful and multiply?

The leaders of the Wiccan community have given us very mixed signals on the issue of magickal ethics. In his book *Incense, Oils, and Brews*, Scott Cunningham lists business incense. The instructions tell the reader to burn the incense in a window to attract customers. Knowing how directly connected the sense of smell is to the brain, this does seem awfully manipulative. Isn't this subliminal advertising, or do subliminal suggestions only count if sight or sound is used? Is there that much difference between the customer attracting incense that Wiccans rarely feel is unethical and the infamous subliminal advertising corporations have been accused of using against unknowing customers? Once you recognize the spell is real and question how it functions, you begin to see how manipulative magick has been a part of Wicca from the very beginning.

Popular false moral: "...and for the good of all and according to free will"

That disclaimer is one of the biggest cop-outs I have ever heard. Is it okay to point a loaded gun at an innocent bystander, tell the bullet not to hit him if he doesn't want it to, and then pull the trigger? The very idea that a few words can excuse our actions is completely contrary to one of the fundamental differences between Wicca and Christianity. Wiccans do not believe that a few words can wash away an unjust action. It doesn't matter if you accept forgiveness or make a confession to your priest. It doesn't matter if you say three Hail Marys afterward or include a disclaimer before. The words and your actions are not the same thing. Whether our actions are physical or magickal makes absolutely no difference. With or without a disclaimer, we are responsible for our own actions. Before placing either physical or magickal action in motion, we must place our brains in gear and decide if that action is something we should do.

Popular false moral: You should never cast a love spell on a particular person because that is robbing their free will

The person who came up with this gem must have checked his reality at the door. If you have a date with a particular person, would it be wrong to prepare a meal that you know she is *particularly* fond of? Is it wrong to take her to a movie that she *particularly* likes? Maybe you overheard her talking to a girlfriend about her favorite scents. Would it be wrong to wear those *particular* scents? If it is not wrong to be *particular* in the real world, then it is not wrong to be *particular* in the magickal world because they are one in the same!

The real threat in casting love spells on a particular person is that you may achieve your goal. When it comes to love, we usually only think we know what we want. More often, it is our whim rather than our will. The result of a successful spell here is missing the lady of your will because you were busy with the lady of your whim.

Love is a curious thing. So much so, that when it comes to magickal ethics, more has probably been written about love spells than spells with any other focus. This is very surprising in a society where it is said that "all is fair in love and war." Again, we see the double standard. Is all fair in love and war except when using magick? How about electricity? All is fair in love and war except when using electricity? What about using fire and gravity?

In Chapter 2, I explained why spells you create tend to work more often than spells you take from a book. I saved a very important point for the discussion of warnings in this chapter. Using a spell you found in book can be very dangerous.

If you are not willing to take the time that is required to research and design your own spells, chances are, you have not taken the time that is required to determine exactly what your intent is. You will be positively miserable when you find out that your spell worked but you didn't really want what you thought you wanted. Acting on your whim with magick is as dangerous as doing the same in the real world because magick is real. How much damage will you do to your credit rating if you impulsively purchase something that you cannot possibly pay for? How much damage would you do to your soul if you fell in love with the wrong person? Before taking any serious action with magick, consider the potential outcome.

Even before considering the outcome of a spell, careful thought should be given to the practice of spellcraft itself. The largest danger in using spellcraft is not in the casting of the spells. It is in the crafting of those spells. Most people are very happy believing the world is as they have been told. They go out of their way to avoid noticing anything that indicates the world is not as it seems to have been painted. To conduct spellcraft properly, you must think outside the box and question what you have been told is reality. People who do so are not generally looked upon fondly.

As you start to observe the world as it really is, you will start to realize it just isn't what we have been told. When you first start observing the pieces that just don't seem to fit, you will be able to turn back, but only if you do so quickly.

If you do turn back, you will probably survive with your mind in tact. But you will never stop wondering what would have happened if you kept going. If you run forward, you may very well become emotionally crippled; you may also become truly great. Sure, you might be completely insane, but it will be an amazing insanity. Besides, once you arrive at the point of insanity, you will realize that sanity is simply a state in which your eyes were shut.

The different potentials depend on your ability to let go of the reality that has already been presented to you. Society has told you that your imaginary friend is not real and that magick is a pipe dream. If you continue to hold onto concern about the way the world appears to be, you will surely go mad because you will see that the world simply is not that way. Your imaginary friend was probably very real and magick is one of the only ways we can explain the tremendous discrepancies between the way the world is and the way the world is perceived.

In a workshop at the Real Witches Ball 2000, Patricia Telesco said that the most powerful magick is love. She wasn't speaking about the kind of love that casual flirts share, she was talking about the kind of love that causes a woman to lift a two ton automobile out of the rut in a railroad track to save her child. Such seemingly impossible acts occur with a frequency that forces us to wonder two things: If not for magick, how was it possible? Why didn't the parent lift the child from the car rather than the car from the rut? The practice of spellcraft includes developing this love.

When Native Americans and U.S. calvary clashed, some Native American tribes would send ghost dancers to the point between the lines. Amidst hails of bullets, these brave souls danced to bring the spirits of their ancestors to the battle. The majority of these great men were not shot while dancing because they trusted wholly that the sacred cloaks of the dance would protect them from all projectiles. The practice of spellcraft includes developing this trust.

How will society perceive you when you can love someone so much that the infidelity cripples you? What will your friends think when you conduct yourself with perfect trust toward a lover that has been unfaithful in the past?

The more spellcraft and magick you incorporate into your life, the more those who do not understand its principles will think you have gone insane. At the point when you wonder if you have crossed the line of sanity, you will have your assurance. You will start to realize exactly how sane you actually are and how crazy the rest of the world is. It is at that point that you will have demonstrated one of the first signs of mental illness: You will believe that you are somehow different from the rest of the world because you and you alone question reality. The secret is, you are not really alone. Society has just wanted you to believe you are so you would turn back.

So, did Pharaoh perform magick when the moon blocked the sun? Maybe and maybe not. Either way, one thing is clear: Pharaoh's ability to predict the moment the moon would pass in front of the sun was determined by someone's inquiry into how solar and lunar orbits work. That is exactly what mastering magick takes: a questioning mind. By questioning an event that you observed, you increase your level of understanding the event. The solar eclipse frightened the ancient people of Egypt because they had not sufficiently questioned the event. They accepted exactly what they were told.

The funny thing about Pharaoh's little trick is that if a slave would have questioned the orbit of the Earth around the sun and the moon around the Earth, the other slaves would have thought he was insane. After all, the reality of the day was that Pharaoh made it happen. The not so funny thing about it is that if that slave had mentioned his questions to one of Pharaoh's priests, the slave would have been put to death.

Things haven't changed much. For the most part, people are still sheep. They are content to believe the world is exactly as they are told. In so doing, they further a *collective reality*, which serves to reinforce the lie of how the world works. It is a classic cycle of victimization that leaves the individual virtually blind to the inconsistencies that point out how false the collective reality actually is. Challenge that view and you are thought to be insane. Do so to anybody that deliberately enforces the lie and you are put to death or otherwise stifled from spreading your inquiry.

With practice, it becomes easy to believe the lies. As a child, how many times were you told that your imaginary friend wasn't real before you started to doubt his existence? You are going to hate me for telling you this, but they lied to you. Your imaginary friend was real and you turned your back on him because some-one *else* didn't believe in him.

When people encounter something that doesn't fit their model of the world, they have three options. They can completely ignore the event, they can notice it but blindly accept that it belongs, or they can question it. Most people will choose without conscious thought. They will automatically ignore or accept that which does not fit the collective reality. A very close friend named SUEZ once expressed this idea by explaining that there are three states in which a human can be found:

1. **Aware**—These are the people who question inconsistencies.
2. **Unaware**—These are the people who notice inconsistencies, but figure reality must be right because there it is.
3. **Unaware of being unaware**—These are the people who just don't notice a thing.

In Nazi-occupied Germany, these three groups could be seen acting accordingly. Group Three didn't notice the genocide. Group Two noticed but figured it was the way of things. Group One formed blocks of resistance.

If there is a gene for awareness, the herd of those who carry that gene has been culled. If it is a matter of nurture, social guidelines have clearly been set; believe what we tell you or you will suffer. This is of particular importance to Wiccans, as the burning times did not develop overnight. Before and after the Church turned its attention to Witches, it had its sights on heretics. Somewhere during the slaughter of millions of people, the lines between Witchcraft and heresy became blurred. At one point, the Spanish Inquisition considered the belief in Witches to be heresy in and of itself. Witches were said to fly, but God had never given anyone the ability to fly. Surely Satan could not give a power that God never offered, so there were no Witches. It didn't matter what religion you were; if you disagreed with the Spanish Inquisition you were usually tortured, tried, and often put to death.

History is filled with other examples of what happens when you do not believe what you have been told. To this day, many people believe Joan of Arc was put to death on a charge of witchcraft. She was officially put to death for the heresy of cross-dressing.

Both the Church and its bible stipulated that women must not wear men's clothing. Joan of Arc questioned that stipulation with both word and action, so Joan of Arc was put to death. Another interesting correlation here is that popular literature also gives the impression that she may have been quite insane.

◆ ◆ ◆

her·e·tic (hr-tk) *n.* A person who holds controversial opinions, especially one who publicly dissents from the officially accepted dogma of the Roman Catholic Church.

(From *The American Heritage Dictionary of the English Language, Third Edition*)

◆ ◆ ◆

Although many people take comfort in the idea that the witch trials and Spanish Inquisition are in humanities distant past, it wasn't long ago that believing the Earth was round or that it rotated around the sun would result in your death. In the last century, questioning Hitler's genocide would result in the same verdict. Today, torture and death are often the rewards of anyone who questions the way dictators run a country. History has shown time and time again that if you ask questions or oppose the generally accepted way of things, you will meet your fate at the hands of those who want to perpetuate the lie. Further, most people will not even think to help you because they have decided to either ignore your persecution, or just accept it as the nature of things. Besides, isn't that someone else's job? Maybe your government's?

On June 4, 1989, in Tiananmen Square, China, hundreds and perhaps thousands of unarmed students and protesters were put to death because they questioned China's communist government. China retained its seat on the United Nations Security Council, the United States and several other nations expanded trade with China, and the same government that mercilessly killed its own people for simply questioning the world in which they lived is now a member of the World Trade Organization. Business as usual.

History has shown that if you question the world in which you live, there is a chance that you will meet a horrible death. Those who have walked that path before you have been burned at the stake, hung, pressed to death, drawn and quartered, gassed, machine gunned, and crucified. The most alarming part of this trend is that the world is mostly populated by people who will do nothing because they are either unaware of your persecution or they think that you must have done something to deserve it.

So why risk it? Because the world needs more Joan of Arcs!

The Chinese government has claimed that 200 students were killed in Tiananmen Square. The United States Secret Service has released documents that put the number as high as 2,600. With this in mind, please ask yourself how important that green money-drawing candle is? Sure, you might need the money. But should it be the focus of almost every spellbook that reports an association to our religion?

Section II

Magick and Spellcraft in Practice

Thar be demons here

Action video games are addictive because they appease cravings for the conquest that the male principle of our soul revels in. When we question the nature of that world, we recognize that it contains the potential of the greatest conquest a man could claim. That is the conquest over those things that are just plain wrong. Although you have the mandate of determining your own ethics, thou art god! As such, your seemingly personal ethics are a very clear manifestation of the Creator's will. Those things that oppose that will are often called the outsiders. They might better be called demons.

Call them demons, outsiders, negative energy, or crimes against humanity; these are the things that we simply do not want in our world. Even when the demons seem fairly small, greater demons continue their onslaught based on the toils of the lesser demons. In the grand scope of things, the conquest over your monthly bills may seem like a battle against fairly small demons. But without the ability to pay your own bills, you cannot move on to combat the giants that cause entire countries to starve.

The three chapters of this section divide intended change into three categories and address each in its own chapter. Chapter 4 discusses the Internal World. This is the place in which we reside. It is everything within our immediate world. It is where we are most comfortable, and it is typically where we require the most change. Here we have the things that we cannot walk away from when we go home because they enter into our home. This is where we encounter our own demons. Some of these demons need to be tamed and some need to be destroyed. Fortunately, most of these demons are fairly small. Unfortunately, they are sometimes hard to find.

Chapter 5 discusses the External World. This is everything outside of your immediate existence. Here the demons are considerably larger. You might think their size would make them easier to locate, but they manage to find some really great hiding places. The worst of all are political parties and huge corporations. Sometimes, entire armies of men have been raised to protect their layers. This makes them much harder to defeat. Some of the wars against these demons have been fought since a time before you or I were born. Fortunately, these are wars that you do not have to fight on your own. In like fashion, the battles have already established victories in which you can revel. This is where the battle against the enslavement of African Americans was won. This is where the suffrage of women was won. This is also the place where the battle against racism wages on with the battle against sexism.

Chapter 6 enters the world of the ether and proposes etheric change. This is where things get tricky. The demons you thought were long since dead return for a final confrontation because you have kept them alive in your thoughts. This is were we confront the molestation and attacks of our childhood. Here is where we transverse time to heal the past and enter your lover's dreams without inhibition or false walls.

With all these demons, it is fortunate that we have structures in which to seek refuge and familiar ground on which to fight. That structure is our religion, whose temples are built on the sacred grounds of our rites. In Section III, you will find recipes and correspondences that will help you transform typical Wiccan rituals into mediums for spellcraft. Please note that due to the diversity of Wiccan customs, the exact format of any Wiccan rite will vary in order and included action from Wiccan to Wiccan and organization to organization. This is intended only as a very brief overview.

General Wiccan ritual format

1. Lustral Bath—Prior to ritual, participants are often asked to bathe with the intent of cleansing the mind, body, and spirit. Most often this will take place in the privacy of each practitioner's home. This is a time of focus and cleansing. If working alone, add herbs that correspond to the god form that you will be calling. If working with a group, have the person who is inviting a god form to do this, but ask the others to bathe with the herbs that correspond to the intent of the rite.

2. Smudging—As ritual begins, the smoke of smoldering sage bundles is often used to further cleanse those in attendance as well as the area in which the rite will be conducted. Try twisting herbs that correspond to your intent into the smudge stick. If you prefer, smudge first with sage and then with an incense blend that corresponds to your intent.

3. The Challenge—Prior to the casting or closing of a Wiccan circle, a challenge must always be given. The idea behind the challenge is to afford everyone in attendance the option of

changing their minds, as all who are in attendance must be there of their own free will. In the case of spellcraft, insure that your challenge is very specific in both format and intent. Including someone who does not share your intent damages your chances of success.

4. Casting of the Circle—This is most often done by one person with an athame to direct energy towards the ground. I prefer to cast the circle twice, once for the Lord and once for the Lady. This is the process of defining the temple, so why not define it in more than just space? The act of casting the circle can also be used to define that circle for intent. Cast your circle as always, but walk it a third time, sprinkling an infusion (tea) made with herbs that correspond to your intent.

5. The Outsider Offering—The outsiders are those forces that we do not want within our circle. In the case of spellcraft, this offering may be used to rid the circle of the forces that would stand in opposition to our intent. Example: If your spell is for a job, try banishing self-doubt in the outsider offering. See your doubt empty into a container, open a gate in your circle, place that doubt outside the circle, and then close the circle. Be vocal at this point; verbal affirmations go a long way.

6. Anointing—Anoint the foreheads of those in attendance with oil that corresponds to the intent. If calling on a specific god form, anoint your forehead with oil that corresponds to that god form. A simple drop of oil at the point of the third eye will do, but the form of the Celtic cross or pentagram is also common.

7. Inviting the Quarters—The Quarters are often invited with their corresponding elements. Some choose to honor each of the Quarters by burning incense that corresponds to its element. Others light color-coordinated candles anointed with the elemental oils. In spellcraft, the words of the invitation should be chosen to reflect the intent of the spell. For example, in a healing rite, one might invite the elements as follows:

East:	Here do I invite Air to lend the breath of life and health.
South:	Here do I invite Fire, like the fever, to burn off the illness that we fight.
West:	Here do I invite Water to wash this illness from the sick.
North:	Here do I invite Earth to provide the firmament on which we will fight this illness.

8. Inviting Our Lord—This is often the single most important part of a Wiccan ritual that is conducted with intent. Choose the archetype in accordance with intent. If you are not comfortable with specific archetypes, call on our Lord in words designed to stimulate those aspects that are aligned with intent. If you are using a candle to represent the archetype being called, anoint that candle with the corresponding oil or use a candle that was made specifically to draw on that god form. In your thoughts and words, remember that you are inviting that god form into yourself. You are asking that you will function with the attributes of that archetype.

9. Inviting Our Lady—Even when a man conducts ritual alone, an invitation to our Lady is also appropriate. In a group setting, it is best to have a woman select an archetype and invite our Lady in much the same way you invite our Lord.

10. Cakes and Ale—This should not be nearly as restrictive as the title sounds. Expand on the idea to include foods and drink that were made with the herbs and spices that correspond to the intent.

11. The spell is cast.

12. Thank our Lord and Lady for attending and for lending their forms to your intent.

13. Thank the Quarters using words appropriate to your intent.

14. Walk the circle counter clockwise, visualizing the energy generated within going forth to fulfill your intent.

Chapter 4

To Cause
Internal Change

Doubt is the antagonist of spellcraft. Not only does it distract from a mental image of success, it enforces an image of failure. This is where social and psychic attacks have taken their toll. If you have been told a thousand times that you cannot accomplish a particular goal, chances are, you won't be able to. Repetition is the key to learning. With each failure, failing will become easier and easier. Like attracts like.

We are not born with doubt. Ask every child in a preschool class who can sing. Hands will fly into the air. Ask them what they can sing, and they will tell you to name the song. It doesn't matter if they know the words, or even the tune, children are absolutely sure they can sing anything you would want. Why? Because nobody has told them they can't. Ask the same question of students in grade school, junior high, and then high school. With each passing year, fewer and fewer hands will go up. By college, the very few that volunteer will put distinct limits on what type of music they can sing.

By the time your intent reaches sufficient maturity, your ability to cause manifestation has fallen victim to fear, doubt, and countless other assaults from the world in which you live. Before you can hope to cause deliberate change outside of yourself, you must first correct the damage that has already been done to your confidence.

While writing this book, I had the great fortune of meeting a young lady who performs with a local theater group. I had never met a professional actor before and used the chance meeting to expand my knowledge. One of my questions was, "What did you want to be when you were 12?" She answered without hesitation, "An actor." I was surprised by her answer. Most people don't follow the profession they sought as a child. "What did your parents think of the idea?" I asked. She told me that when she was 12, they encouraged her dream. But by the time she entered high school, her parents' encouragement changed to, "you should prepare for a *real* job." Without training or practice, she was able to accomplish what counselors and psychologists often fail to do. She was able to break the cycle of victimization.

Because we cannot turn off our minds, our natural state is to be the victim of everything we observe. Anything that you see or otherwise sense has already entered your mind. Once there, the thought behind that observation will manifest in one way or the other. This is one of the reasons perpetrators of domestic violence are often victims of domestic violence. Those who commit sex crimes are often the victims of sex crimes.

As adults, we must face the cold reality that such assaults are not excuses. We are responsible for our own actions and inactions. If you grew up surrounded by domestic violence, I am sorry. But that does not excuse your acts of domestic violence. If you were molested as a child, I am also sorry. But that does not excuse your acts of molestation. If you grew up in a society that did not get involved, I am sorry. But that does not excuse your inactions.

Unintentional attacks are the most common. But even when the attack is not deliberate, our minds observe and then try to manifest what it has observed. The largest source is parents, friends, and peers. Someone prevented them from trying, so they attempt to prevent you. They probably have the best of intentions. Maybe they think they are saving you the pain of disappointment. What they are really doing is programming you to fail.

How many times has someone told you that your dreams are unrealistic? How many times have your parents or friends attempted to protect you from failure by convincing you not to try? An inaction is in and of itself an action, so if you do not try, you have already failed. When it comes to spellcraft, if you grew up surrounded by failure, I am sorry. But that absolutely does not excuse your failure!

There are also deliberate attacks. Advertising agencies are predominantly responsible for these. You can't turn on the television or read a magazine without being told you are not whole without one product or the next. The hair and diet industries just love to generate a poor self-image. That way they can sell you products to fix what might be an entirely contrived problem. If you listen long enough, you will start to believe everyone is as superficial as the advertisement implies.

> "Does your wife really love you even though you are going bald? Buy our new *Hair in a Can* and get rid of those doubts once and for all."

> "Ted here lost 500 pounds this summer by eating our sandwiches. Now he's a babe magnet. Maybe your life would be better if you ate what Ted eats."

Around every corner we hear that our head is too bald and our stomachs are too big. Spam (unsolicited commercial e-mail) is even worse. If you have an e-mail account, I am sure you have been told that your penis is too small. Of course there is a cure for each and every problem they say you have, but you will just have to purchase a product or visit a Web site. Have your credit card ready. The worst part about the commercial assaults is that they are very well targeted. They know that men are more concerned about mating habits, so that's where they focus their attention. Even though e-mail is free, America Online accounts that are listed as belonging to men will receive a much greater amount of spam from porn sites.

> "Want more women? Try our new stud in a can. Finally, the pheromones she can't resist are just $39.95. Guaranteed or your money back!"

Will they also return your self-esteem? The world has pounded us so long that it's no wonder we manifest self-doubt. It must be the way someone wants it to be. After all, just about the entire corporate world wants to keep the ball rolling right along. Even the companies who claim they are concerned with our sanity do everything they can to injure our mental health.

> "Ask your doctor if the blue pill is right for you."

Just in case you have a tiny sense of self-reliance left, the pharmaceutical companies are at hand to rip it from your soul. Maybe you are not whole without the latest antidepressants. Why would anyone ask a doctor about a cure when he is not sick? Because the commercials will cause you to doubt that you are well.

Of course there are clear circumstances where antidepressants are helpful. If you are riddled with depression, antidepressants will make you feel a lot better. They won't stop the self-doubt, but after a week or two you won't care. If used properly, they can help you shift your focus away from the depression so your counselor can help you heal.

Other drugs are also useful to distract the mind from the problem long enough to make repairs. If you are bleeding to death, morphine will make you feel a lot better. It won't stop the bleeding, but after a shot or two you just won't care. If used properly, it can help you shift your focus away from the injury so medics can stop the bleeding.

Both antidepressants and morphine are useful to the healing process when they are used correctly. Both can be very dangerous to your health if they are used incorrectly. However, I have never seen a commercial advertising the latest designer morphine. Some people do have chemical imbalances that need to be addressed, but "mystery drug" commercials are not aimed at the sick; they are aimed at the healthy for the purpose of causing psychosomatic illness. Each is its own little magickal attack on your mind for the purpose of profit.

No matter what you do, you will continue to receive these assaults. You can turn off your television. You can move away from environments that are not conducive to your health. You can stop listening to people who bring you down, but you cannot prevent every potential attack, so you must establish walls to stave off those attacks.

"Throw the circle thrice about to keep unwelcome spirits out"
—*from the Poem of the Wiccan Rede*

Wiccan rituals imitate life. Where the circle is cast, a boundary of sacred space is defined. Everything within the circle is separated from the rest of the world. The body has a very similar boundary of sacred space. This border between our internal and external world is seen by most children. When young folk draw living things, they often include a glow around the body. The most devout spiritual leaders are often painted with this boundary clearly defined as a radiant field around their bodies. Sometimes this brilliance is concentrated around the head, producing the halo that is seen in classic Western imagery of holy men. This boundary is typically called the aura.

Classic art can be used to establish aura lore. It has been called the nimbus, glory, mandorla, and other names. By each name, two very distinct guidelines can be established. The first is that the aura tends to concentrate itself around the head. The second is that the aura becomes more intense with greater levels of spirituality.

Remembering that religion and magick are not the separate things that the Western world has insisted, you can see the significance of the association between the aura and levels of magickal skill. The greater our mind becomes, the more intense our aura becomes.

The aura is very real. It can be photographed, measured, and quantified. But there is absolutely no evidence that it has the ability to protect the mind or body any better than a circle on the ground. Each is a tool for visualization; it is your intent that brings the protection of both the circle and your aura. In the case of the aura, the intensity is an indication of your spiritual/magickal development. The greater your mind becomes the more intense your aura becomes. Your aura is a method of measuring your ability to protect your mind and body.

To strengthen the aura

An excellent way to extend and strengthen your aura is to improve the working of your chakras. If you are not familiar with the chakras and their relation to this practice, I suggest you read *Pocket Guide to Crystals and Gemstones,* by Sirona Knight. It should be noted that, although the external location of the root chakra is between the genitals and the anus, for the purpose of this exercise, we treat the root chakra as if it were found at the soles of the feet.

If you have someone you trust intimately, invite her to help you with this rite. Intimacy is important because it is just about necessary to be sky clad in this rite. With this chant, cast your circle and erect the temple as normal, except, instead of channeling energy with an athame, scatter salt as you visualize the creation of your circle, and smudge with very liberal amounts of protection incense.

"Aura strong and aura bright
I'm guarded with protective light."

With the circle cast, lie down with your face to the sky or ceiling. It is a good idea to incorporate a comfortable sleeping pad or even a bed into this rite if you have the space. If you are working with a partner, have her anoint your chakras. If not, anoint them yourself. In either case, use the soles of your feet as the root chakra. If available, anoint the chakras with corresponding chakra oil. If any of the seven different chakra oils are not available, substitute almond oil for all of the oils. If working with a partner, have her follow a modified version of the chant.

"Aura strong and aura bright

You're guarded with protective light."

If you are working with a partner, have her continue the chant as she places stones on each of your center five chakras and on the floor just beyond your root (feet) chakra and crown (top of the head) chakra in accordance with the following chart:

Semiprecious Minerals and the Meditative Chakras

Chakra	Best choice	Second choice
Crown	Rutilated Quartz	Herkimer Diamond
Third Eye	Sugilite Star	Sapphire in matrix
Throat	Lapis Lazuli	Sodalite
Heart	Malachite	Adventurine
Solar Plexus	Citrine (yellow/golden)	Tourmaline or Tourmalated Quartz
Sacral	Fluorite (orange)	Bloodstone
Root	Hematite	Agate (red or blood)

Continuing the chant, you partner should use the stones to massage each of the chakras. Starting with the feet, she should lightly rub the stones in a clockwise movement. As she works her way to your crown, she should alternate the direction of the circles with each chakra, visualizing the energy moving up from each of the chakras as it begins to spin with her motion. As more and more chakras spin, see the energy rising from your feet and looping between the chakras.

As this energy leaves your body at the crown chakra, see it rise from your head and then cascade down your body in all directions, as if you were a standing fountain. At your base, see the energy re-enter the body at the feet. As you continue this meditation, your partner can open the temple as normal, or you can once you have completed the meditation.

Strengthening the aura as a daily practice

See your aura extend half the normal conversational distance for your culture. In the United States, this is the point that is just slightly out of range of a thrown fist. I found the distance to be much shorter while in Europe. Be aware of this boundary and make others aware of that boundary. This is the sacred space in which your body resides. If someone enters that space without invitation, don't try to explain the aura or your personal sacred space, just tell her you are uncomfortable with her gesture.

Because like attracts like, there is no better way to strengthen the boundaries of your personal sacred space than by respecting the personal sacred space of others. If you wish to enter another person's sacred space, obtain permission first. Ideally, this permission will take the form of spoken words. However, clearly understood gestures can be just as effective if everyone is honest in his intent. You should not hug someone without their permission; however, you do not have to verbally ask them for permission. Instead, you can hold out your arms in a gesture and they can choose to either refuse the gesture or walk into your arms and return it.

If you feel utterly uncomfortable rejecting an offered hug, then take the person's hands and thank him for the affection offered. If even this seems too close, cross those hands as you take them. This gives the illusion of closeness while making it clear that you have limits.

To further strengthen the aura

At night, outside, unarmed, and in a place that you do not know, sit alone. Listen to the night. Remember that you are human. As such, you have no natural weapons or camouflage. You can't run fast or jump high and your night vision is poor compared to the critters that are watching you from behind the darkness.

Once you realize that you should be concerned about your safety, but not before, build a small fire. Use dead fall from ash, cedar, and/or oak if you can. There is no reason to harm a tree to heal a human. As you meditate, sprinkle a combination of dragon's blood, frankincense, and lavender onto the coals. Ideally, you will want three ounces of dragon's blood, three ounces of frankincense, and nine ounces of lavender, because it is going to be a very long night. Unfortunately, dragon's blood can be very expensive so purchase what seems reasonable. Make sure you break up the dragon's blood beforehand or purchase it as a powder. If you cannot have an open fire, you can bring a fire container with you, start it with coal, and then toss oak chips onto the coals. During the Summer, oak chips are readily available at most grocery stores. Boil some green tea, chamomile, and/or sage over the fire, and sweeten it with cane sugar.

Bring with you a meal that contains, or was prepared with, any combination of basil, bay, beans, caraway seeds, cinnamon, clove, cumin, dill, hazelnuts, onions, olives, and olive oil. Use enough of the spices that there will be a very distinct odor.

Focus on the resins melting into the coals. See your aura as a ring of fire surrounding you, protecting you from forces that would do you harm.

"Aura strong and aura bright,

Build this wall I need tonight,

Fire burn and fire sing,

From the night protection bring."

Chant until the fire goes out and then sleep under the stars. So mote it be.

Simple spells for protection

Spells do not need to be complicated or conducted within circle to be effective. Even the simplest of charms can be tremendously useful. Fill a sachet with protection incense (see Chapter 7 and use juniper berries). Add a piece of tiger's eye and charge with intent:

> "Bag of berries, root and stone
> Keep me safe while I'm alone."

Even with the strongest aura and best talisman, you cannot allow yourself to be abused. It is easy to turn away a stranger, but acquaintances that rob your energy and drag your mood into the ground should also be alerted to your limits. Even if they maintain a proper physical distance, your other senses will open the door to your mind. Sight, sound, and smell will slice right through your defenses.

You know who these people are. They always have a story to tell and it is never pleasant. They spread doubt and fear (two of the most dangerous thoughts to the aura), and generally destroy a good disposition. Call them social vampires, drama queens, antagonist, or abusers; but do not call them friend, partner, and, for the love of the gods, do not call them lover.

> "With a fool no season spend, lest be counted as his friend."
> —*from the poem of the Wiccan Rede*

If they cannot respect your limits, your best course of action is to modify your life in a manner in which you are not exposed to abusive people. Unfortunately, this is not always possible. When it is not, know your limits and do not approach them. When you think you have taken about half of what you are able, then ground it out.

Once our protection is in place, it is time to cast out those things that were already inside: our outsiders.

Banishing (getting rid of the outsiders)

The outsider ritual is a great way to banish fear, confusion, cowardice, weakness of the mind, self-doubt, and the general blues/bad vibes. Anoint the inside of a fire-safe bowl with banishing oil. Write down the things that you want to remove from your life and place the paper inside the bowl. Sprinkle the paper with a few more drops of banishing oil and set it on fire. As it burns, repeat these words and visualize the outsiders being drawn from your abdomen up and out of your body at the mouth.

"Fear and weakness
Confusion and doubt
I draw you up
I cast you out!"

Carry the oil with you for the last two weeks of a lunar cycle. At the top of each waking hour, put a drop on the area of your body where the outsiders dwell, and rub the oil in as you drive the outsiders out with the chant.

Whenever you brush your teeth, think of the outsiders when you rinse. See them swelling up inside you, leaving your mouth with the rinse water, and spiraling down the drain afterward.

To keep a secret

Place a drop of Horus oil on your left wrist and a drop of diluted camphor oil on your right wrist. Hold your left palm to the sun and your right to the Earth. Imagine the secret coming from the sun, traveling through your body without stop, and then joining the Earth.

"My lips are sealed my faith is strong
My urge to tell will not last long."

To improve leadership skills

This is especially useful if you lead any group, organization, or business where subordinates invoke artistic abilities.

Burn Apollo incense and see yourself as the conductor of a grand symphony as you chant:

"Muse my heart and muse my mind

Let my muse respond in kind."

To become forceful

This can be used anywhere there is not a more specific spell.

With Ares incense burning and the temples anointed with Ares oil, drip dragon's blood perfume oil on a sword. Stand and repeat:

"My sword is strong,

My sword is wet

My sword is drawn,

I'm not done yet."

Do this enough in the privacy of a solitary circle, and when it is time to invoke this mantra in the real world, you words can be spoken internally and you will need neither sword or oil.

To heal a broken heart

Is it better to have loved and lost? Of course it is! But that doesn't make the pain of loss hurt any less. Brahma oil can. Use it no more than one lunar cycle after losing your love and use it only when that loss was her doing. Before each meal, place three drops on your right palm, then slap your palms together such that a loud clap can be heard and announce to the world that "I am whole!"

Without her, you can concentrate on finding the partner that is right for you. Repeat these words to the image as if it were that person. On the last day, burn the image or bury the doll. If you can get to a flowing body of water, toss it in and then watch as the image is taken as far from you as possible.

"With my heart I was so blind

Now true love my heart can find."

To bring on courage and bravery

This is especially useful in easing paranoia and promoting the awareness necessary to determine actual threat levels. It lowers feelings of guilt caused by action, but will increase the feelings of guilt by inaction. If you are not willing to do something about a situation, then your actions ask for that guilt, and neither this oil nor a year with a shrink will help that (see also banishing oil).

When you want to confront a fear, determine exactly when the confrontation will be (best when the moon is full). Each night for two weeks before that day, diffuse courage oil into the air while reciting the chant as long as you can. Then carry the oil with you when it is time for a confrontation; place several drops on the palm of your projective hand. Rub your hands together firmly to distribute the oil and generate heat. Cup your hands over your nose and mouth (do not touch your face). Recite the chant into your hands until you feel ready.

> "By my body, by my heart
> By my soul, by my mind
> By this fear that's really not
> But a wasting but my time."

Achieving balance in your soul

Joke: How many New Agers does it take to screw in a light bulb?

When you think of finding balance in your soul, chances are, you think of some fluffy New Age ceremony that involves sitting in the Lotus position and holding a crystal in each hand. My old knees won't even bend in that direction, which is a good thing because, after wrecking my Harley, one of them bent in every other direction. So, how many New Agers does it take to screw in a light bulb? None, they just think happy happy thoughts into their crystals until they glow.

If you have spent any time in the New Age/quasi-neopagan portion of our community, chances are, you have been hugged so many times that you have almost forgotten your right to refuse such things. We have been fed so much white light that sometimes it is hard to enter a New Age bookstore without a pair of dark sunglasses. I once merchanted at a white light convention. After two days of white light, nothing would calm my nerves short of dark beer.

Balance is achieved by placing equal forces on both sides of a fulcrum. A 200-pound man cannot play seesaw with a child. Two men of equal weight cannot play if they sit on the same side of the seesaw.

Balance with Noise

Make a model of whatever it is that has caused the tension to build, the more lifelike in size, the better. If it is a person, find out what that person's zodiac sign is. If it is a corporation, then make a doll that represents the attributes that have affected you. Maybe you think someone has played a horrible trick on you; buy a coyote doll (the trickster). Maybe you think someone has operated mindlessly, as if his or her brain were inside a cardboard box. Then use a doll whose head is enclosed in a cardboard box. Fill the doll or whatever represents the force that contributed to your imbalance with the herbs and stones that best represent the force you want to remove. Don't visualize the victim as being the person or organization itself. Instead, see the doll as that influence on your soul and your soul's willingness to accept the abuse.

Throw back some red wine (alcohol free will do if you must); anoint the doll with Dionysus oil. Call his spirit into your body. Drop the doll to the ground and punt it as far as you can. Run to it as fast as you can and punt it again. Do this over and over, again and again until you can run no more without a break and then fall to the ground, recover the doll, and rip it to pieces.

If you want to make sport of this practice, gather men of similar tension and use a life size doll. Make the doll sturdy enough to be hung and use it as a punching bag. When the first man gets tired enough, he should scream the name Dionysus, and then all partake in ripping the doll apart.

Balance with Quiet

Then there is the Real Witches Ball. Each year, thousands of pagans descend on my neighborhood from around the world. The event fills three days of sleeplessness and consumes three months with planning, cleaning, and making the many things that I have to sell at the event to pay for the thing. The store is not open for a few days after the event because we must find balance in the quiet of solitude.

A gentle massage from a lover will help obtain this balance, but if there is any possible chance that your exchange will involve even one word, do not accept the offer. Your rite should be absolutely silent, free of all distractions. Unplug everything you own, including telephone and lights. Use only candlelight.

Draw a warm bath into which you should toss sea salt and a few drops of water oil. Burn water incense with your candle. See the warm water drawing out the tension and drowning the noise. When you are finished, watch the tub drain and see your stress and noise draining with it.

In a different room, outside if you can, burn Earth incense and massage Earth oil into your feet. Stand barefoot on the Earth if you can. Feel the noise falling through your body and entering the Earth at the point where you and she meet. Once all that noise is either down the drain or in the Earth, go into your bedroom to sleep on lavender-filled pillows.

Protecting the home (especially when you are leaving loved ones there)

If you are the oldest man of your home who is concerned with such matters, the duty of protecting that home falls to you. Remember that the ritual circle is a sacred space that represents the home, but this is the real thing. Cast a circle around your domain and mark the Quarters with stones; large flat ones are the best, as they make wonderful tables for offerings. On each stone, burn the incense that corresponds to the Quarter's element. If the weather conditions are right, anoint a candle of the appropriate color with the corresponding oil, and light it as you invite the elements of each Quarter to watch over your domain in the way you would invite them to watch over a rite:

"East and Air hear me out
Wrap your breath around my doubt."

"South and Fire find me now
Harm to these do not allow."

"West and Water come to me
Bring to these your harmony."

"North and Earth come this way
Protect these folk night and day."

Taking a hint from wolves and other natural creatures, mark your territory with urine. Step just beyond each of your Quarter stones and relieve yourself.

To improve your relationships

Mother

Bring her a dozen yellow roses on a day that she would not ordinarily expect a gift. I say bring them, not send them, because before you give them to her, you should use an exacto knife and carefully remove each and every thorn. Add a drop of Cupid oil to the flower of each rose, then one for luck. Surprise your mother with the gift and then flush the thorns down her toilet without her knowledge.

Wife

Do the same as for the mother, only bring red roses and leave the thorns in tact. A little pain is a natural part of youth and growth.

Wife and Mother

Sometimes they team up on you. If that is the case, bring roses of appropriate colors but lace each with Adonis oil.

Others relationship(s) involving love of any kind

Pick an appropriate gift of an appropriate color, and then scent it with Eros oil.

Prosperity

In all acts where the intent is prosperity, remember that the path of receiving is cleared by the act of giving. If you do just what is expected of you at work, you will receive just what you expect in the prosperity department. However, if you give it your all and blast that path open, when it is time for a raise, the path leading back to your wallet will be clear.

Prosperity is sometimes elusive in a system where almost everything can be broken down into cash figures. This is because the universe does not have an accountant to keep track of the conversions. Our spells act on our intent. Although we may think that intent is for a cash return, more often, our true intent is for something far less tangible. You may think you want money when your true intent is to find a home for the family you hope to build. Discovering that intent will greatly improve your chances of recognizing success in your spells for prosperity.

Real prosperity does not refer to figures in a bank account, because those figures are not manifest. Those figures are just the idea of prosperity. Yes, money is often needed to acquire our true intent, but focusing on the money itself will limit your intent greatly. If you are cold and think your intent is to acquire a blanket, do not limit your magick by focusing on the blanket when changing the weather will have even better results.

The single best way to become prosperous is to discover your creative passions. Your drive to be successful will be increased a thousandfold by focusing on something you are motivated to succeed at. This is not always your current job. If you want to work with flowers, fixing cars is just not going to get you to your goals, even if it does pay three times the salary of a florist.

Do burn prosperity incense in your spells and meditations, but unless you already know what it is that fires your heart, do not focus on receiving cash. Instead, focus on discovering the path to your prosperity. Find out what will cause your soul to force your success and then focus on manifesting that which you discover is your true intent. Toward that goal, you have several friends and allies (see Chapter 9).

If you have trouble determining your intent, try calling on Hades in your rites. You might be hung up on the idea that he was the guardian of the underworld, but remember that the underworld is where many of life's riches are found. He is also a very decisive god; he often knows in an instant what others take lifetimes to discover.

Add to your ritual fire an ample amount of brimstone (sulfur), stoke your sensor with his incense, and anoint your body with his oils. Dance around the fire to raise your heart as you chant his call:

> "Brimstone fire burning hot
> True intent discovered not!
> Hades! Hades! Forget me not!"

Friends and allies in prosperity

Like attracts like does not just mean you should use money in money-drawing spells. It means you should use like souls in soul-drawing spells. If you want to be rich, befriend someone with money and take him out to lunch. Guess who picks up the check: You do. After all, it is you who are there to learn. If you want to be successful, spend time with people who are successful. Keep in mind that possession of one desirable attribute does not mean that other attributes will not be less desirable. Choose your friends and influences carefully.

Of the people you will see on a regular basis, make a list of the people you admire and people that you do not. Arrange the names on that list in order of influence. Leave the centermost position empty. To the left and right of the centermost position, place people whose influence you desire the most. On the outermost edge of your peripheral vision, place the images of those whose influences you desire the least. Make it a game. Each time you see a positive influence, put them in the center of your vision. Each time you see a negative influence, put them in the peripheral of your vision. As you add people to the center, they push the peripherals out of your range of vision. As you place people on the peripherals, they push people inward. Remove anyone that is pushed to the center position. Try to finish each day with no one on your imaginary scenery of influence except good influences. Ultimately, it is your soul. You can use it to take what life gives you or take what you want from life.

Nothing says these figures have to be human. Our heritage and mythology is full of role models on which to base deliberate peer pressure. We have god forms, elements, models of our power center, and more lore than one could possibly learn in a single lifetime. Many of these models have plants, scents, gemstones, and other associations that can be used to trigger their archetype within you (see Chapter 9).

Apollo

Apollo and prosperity are associated in all matters of the arts. He was once in charge of the Muses, and although he no longer works in that capacity, he still has a few friends in the business that he can call to your aid. His main focuses are pottery and fine arts, so if your plan is to sell laser color copies, you might want to skip giving him a call. With his incense burning on an altar decorated with tourmaline and sapphire, call him with your heart and with your own words.

Ganesa

If you have pet rats, I have found some of the best spells to draw prosperous pattern involve these cute little critters. Burn Ganesa incense and feed your critters a few peanuts. Don't have rats? Put some of his oil on your wrists and take it to the road. Just about every town has a pet store these days.

If you call him directly, do not do so except with joy and with dance, for that is his nature. Lace your fire with ample amounts of peanut oil and invite only your joyful friends. If you can deal with the mirth, you could even play the *Baby Elephant Walk* by Henry Mancini, but that might force you to dance the Baby Elephant Dance as well. Don't know what the Baby Elephant Dance is? Don't worry, light the fire, play the music, and you will.

"Long of trunk and long of mirth
Dancer large upon the Earth
Fortune here we now desire
So we call with your own fire."

We entered Section II with a warning that "Thar be demons here"; it is only appropriate that we leave this chapter with the Baby Elephant Dance dance on our mind. So mote it be!

Chapter 5

To Cause External Change

Thar be big demons here

I f you attempt to cause external change, you will quickly learn that some will oppose your intent. Sometimes the opposition will take the form of physical violence. One of the greatest Witches of all times had some interesting things to say of this matter. He instructed that when you are struck on your cheek, you should turn and offer the other. Christ was not instructing you to take abuse; he was instructing you to fight back intellectually. At the time, a Roman could slap a slave with the backside of his hand. To slap him with the inside of the palm was to acknowledge the slave as an equal. There was no crime in slapping a slave, but there was in slapping an equal. Because the left hand was never used for anything more elevated than wiping one's posterior, this forced the Roman to either stop the assault, or treat the victim as an equal. Likewise, the instruction to carry a soldier's pack beyond what was expected was intended to shame the soldier. In either case, when we examine the words of our brother Christ from a Gnostic eye, we recognize the greatness His story reveals.

If you don't like hearing about Christ in a book on Wicca, you had better not go on to your next step in spiritual evolution. The latest guesswork is that there is about one half million Wiccans in the United States alone. Sound like a large number? If they are telling us the truth, there are about six billion people in this world that are not Wiccan. There is tremendous strength in numbers. If we want to achieve external change, we must recognize that strength and get over our childish prejudices.

I am amazed and baffled at how many Wiccans try to cast spells completely uninhibited by the laws of physics and the other natural laws that science has uncovered. Setting aside the very obvious magickal guideline that there is strength in numbers, there are still thousands upon thousands of obvious guidelines that are also ignored. Throwing a snowball at a tank just doesn't produce dramatic results. If you want to get rid of that tank, try climbing the mountain next to it and rolling a snowball towards the tank. Remember that one war cry is all it takes to cause an avalanche.

You can cause tremendous external change with this same principle. Of course, you do not have to bellow that war cry. You can continue to dwell in the pagan community and absorb all of the free love and goddess healing that you desire. If that's your choice, you will probably agree with Janis Joplin: "Freedom is just another word for nothing less to lose."

I say freedom has no value without the liberty to use it. Without liberty, you are still a slave. Dwell in the house of freedom without waging the constant war for liberty if that is your intent, but don't think you are anything more than a slave in a fancy cage. And above all, remember that you do so at the suffering of those who are willing to fight at the battle lines of liberty.

"Eternal vigilance is the price of liberty." That quote is commonly attributed to Thomas Jefferson, but it is more likely that the exact wording was first spoken by Wendell Phillips before the Massachusetts Antislavery Society in 1852. When you consider the real origin of the quote, know that there is only one God and that God has been seen by many eyes in many ways and has been given many names.

♦ ♦ ♦

"The condition upon which God has given liberty to man is eternal vigilance." —John Philpot Curran: Speech upon the Right of Election, July 10, 1710

♦ ♦ ♦

Christian, Muslim, Pagan, Jew, our God is the same; Lord of Lords, God of Gods!

You do not have to live in the wonderful country in which I find myself, but it does make it easier to point out how lazy we have become. The students in Tiananmen Square, China, stood for liberty. In a country with a totalitarian government, it was easy to put down the uprising with machine-gun fire. But in the United States, and other places where freedom has been won, many of us are willing to sit back with our Janis Joplin records, content in the illusion that we are free.

Janis Joplin may have sung "Freedom is just another word for nothing less to lose," but such advice is best taken only by those who are too stoned to realize they can manifest change. When you are truly free, there is always something left to lose.

I say:

"Gay, straight, black, white
Same struggle, same fight!"

A popular protest chant whose origins I cannot trace:

"Christian, Muslim, Pagan, Jew
Just one world for me and you!"

My addition to the chant. Read them together:

"Gay, straight, black, white
Same struggle, same fight
Christian, Muslim, Pagan, Jew
Just one world for me and you!"

Can your voice be heard? Can you make a difference? Did you ever think you would read someone's quotes about the Christian god in a book on Wiccan spellcraft? Did you ever read such dedication to events that took place in a nonreligious communist country in a religious book written in a democratic country? Yes, you can still listen to your Janis Joplin records. I love her music myself. But don't forget that anything earned feels tremendously better than anything given.

"Deosil go by the waxing moon, singing out ye Witches' Rune"
—*from the poem of the Wiccan Rede*

Deosil means clockwise. It isn't just the direction in which we cast our circles, it is one of the two directions we can turn the knobs on a stereo system. Sometimes we turn it counterclockwise for introspect and the volume goes down. When we are trying to cause external change, it is time to turn it clockwise. So let's fire up the Mars incense, turn up the volume, and get this thing in gear.

We are winning the war in which the Church state insisted that men have dominion over animals; the Wiccan ethic that animals have soul is spreading. When Christians call on their bible to justify cock fighting, judges are throwing them into jail. It doesn't matter if the judge, the court, or even the people who voted for the law do not call themselves Wiccan; it is our ethic that is winning. Call it Wicca or call it purple bubble gum, it does not matter if we win!

In order to cause external change, you must first identify what it is that you want to change. There is a magickal teaching that says when you know a thing's true name, then you have power over it. If that true name is its description, that magickal teaching is correct. This is the process of determining its strengths and weaknesses.

Chances are, if you feel there is a need to cause external change, someone else has felt the same way and has formed an organization for that purpose. There is strength in numbers. Your contacts do not need to call themselves Wiccan or even pagan. You will know their hearts by their actions. If a man's heart is pagan, the declaration need not be spoken for his deeds to talk.

Contact those organizations and follow their instructions, as well as contacting every form of the press that you can imagine, including television, radio, and print. Find the time and place to hold a grand circle and use the curiosity of the press to get your message out.

Ideally, each spell will be cast at, or as close as possible, to what you seek to protect. If there is any question as to the legality of your assembly, get all necessary permissions and paperwork. Always contact the local law enforcement agencies by certified letter containing contact information, as well as information concerning the location, nature, and time of the rite. Keep a copy of the letter and staple the proof of delivery to it. They should be able to judge what type of protection you will need because that is their job.

Post Quarter guards in each of the directions. Arm those Quarter guards with copies of all paperwork necessary to prove that not only do you have the legal right to conduct the rite at that site, but that notification was sent to the authorities prior to the rite. Include also a list of every organization you have contacted about the situation you wish to change, and include that contact information in the bundle of paperwork. Arm the Quarter guards with those papers and nothing else except the oils and incenses of the elements with which their Quarters are associated. Before the rite begins, the Host and Hostess of the event should give everyone a copy of all paperwork along with contact information. This includes everyone participating or watching the rite, as well as all members of the press that might show up.

When those Quarters are called, the Quarter guards are to face the direction of the Quarter, invite the corresponding elements using words that are applicable to the specific rite, and then end with "So mote it be." Everyone in the circle should then repeat "so mote it be." The Quarter guards *do not* turn to face the rite. Their job is to protect the rite, not watch it. If anyone attempts to disrupt the rite, the Quarter guard has the responsibility of using the weapons he has been given, and nothing more, to stave off the attack.

Have every member of the circle come with a typed letter about whatever it is that you seek to change, but tell them not to sign it. During the rite, preferably with drumming in the background, have each come forward and sign the letters. Have them sign each letter with a normal fountain pen so that they will look normal, but replace the ink with dragon's blood ink. Have them also address their envelopes in their own hand with the same pen. Keep extra envelopes on hand for mistakes. Seal the envelopes and set them in a basket for charging. Mail them as soon as you can after the rite.

When you interview with the press, be ready to explain exactly why the rite was performed and provide the names and phone numbers of those you have contacted ready. Refuse to be interviewed without the promise that your interviewer will show the phone numbers for the national organizations that you contacted. Get that promise in writing. If they fail to follow their promise, demand that they place your complaint in their public file, and contact the Federal Communication Commission (in the case of radio and television) to insure that it was indeed placed there.

To protect natural habitat and wildlife

When you find a natural habitat in danger, contact the National Wildlife Federation and other similar organizations to determine exactly what to do and to whom to write.

Praise our Lord Agni, the Hindu embodiment of plants, fertility, and male vitality. His element is the element of war itself: Fire! Drown your flesh with his oil and burn his incense in great billows of smoke. Coat your tools and fill your thurbles with his blood (dragon's blood resin and perfume oil).

Dance the circle deosil and chant out his name, his lore, and his praise:

"Lord of lords and lord of light
Save this land and bless this rite."

To protect domestic animals

When we consider the word *humane*, we can see just how pompous and self-centered our species can be. I can think of no creature that can be more inhumane than those who claim its namesake, humans. Fortunately, for the hordes of people who haven't heard the pagan ethic that animals have souls, we have the Humane Society of the United States and its associations around the world. When you find domestic animals in danger, contact the Humane Society and other similar organizations to determine exactly what to do and to whom to write.

This rite should be conducted in two circles under a full moon. For 24 hours prior to the rite, everyone should abstain from all food and drink except for wine. Non-alcohol wine is probably best to keep a fairly clear head. Whenever you have an urge to eat anything, purchase or otherwise secure the food and save it for the rite. The inner circle should be formed by everyone who participates without a dog or wolf-like animal. The outer circle should be formed by everyone who participates with their dog or wolf-like animal on a leash or tether short enough to maintain control. The outer circle must be sparse enough that no two animals can reach each other even if both leashes are extended fully. If the circle is not that sparse, expand it. If this is the first time the animals have been in circle, insure that all animal handlers understand that they are responsible for the animal they brought.

Arm the Quarter guards and distribute the pertinent literature as discussed earlier. Stoke your thurble with Odin incense or oak. Anoint everyone and every animal at the point where the back joins the neck. It is a very good idea for the animal handlers to do the anointing previously. For this rite, everyone in the outer circle should sign and seal their letters ahead of time. Those envelopes should already be at the center altar in a basket but the letters written by those in the inner circle should still be unsigned.

Praise our All Father Odin and his friends Freki and Geri. The outside circle faces inward and the inside circle faces outward. The outside circle of people remain silent while the inside circle starts the rite by screaming the name of the All Father in an easier tongue, "WoooooooooooTaaaaaaaaaaaaaaan," over and over again until the animals join your scream.

Continue the scream as everyone from the inner circle signs their letters one by one and then seals the envelopes and places them in the basket. As they do, continue the chant for the background, but add to it a drum beat, and the following chant. Once the letters have all been signed, sealed, and placed in the basket, this chant should be repeated by everyone within the inner circle while the "Wotan" chant continues in the outer circle.

"Father good and Father fine
Father all and Father mine
Friend of wolf and of canine
Take this food on which we dine."

The inner circle should then offer the saved food to the animals in the outer circle. Rather than feeding them by hand, place the food on the ground and back away. Allow the animal's keeper to let the animal advance on the food after you have withdrawn. It is entirely possible the animal will have enough exuberance that he might confuse your hand for his supper. Remember, Odin's death was predicted to come at the mouth of a wolf.

To protect liberty (as expressed in the U.S. Bill of Rights)

In the United States, religious freedom is guaranteed under the same portion of the Bill of Rights as freedom of the press. This is a wonderful fact to present to the press when attempting to secure their involvement in any form of discrimination, but particularly in the case of religious discrimination.

The problem with that association is that, often times, the press is in the pockets of the authorities. Gone are the days when every town had at least two competing newspapers trying desperately to scoop each other. Now many towns have one newspaper that takes whatever table scraps the authorities have to offer because they are afraid if they push for more they will be treated poorly. Television and radio aren't much better. Yes, there is competition, but ratings pay the bills and ratings are determined more by breasts, contests, and entertainment than by reporting the actual news.

When it comes to matters of liberty, the U.S. Wiccans have no larger tool than the American Civil Liberties Union. Add to this our political system, and there is virtually no religious discrimination that cannot be arrested in its tracks. The trick is stirring these forces to rally behind our cause. If that cause is true and just, most will join in.

In the case of governmentally sponsored harassment, there is an interesting little feature about the U.S. political system that can be exploited. Many politicians are also members of the American Bar Association. Although it's hard to believe from the conduct among a few of these folks, they are held to a higher level of ethics than most people. The American Bar Association tends to frown on lawyers who speak out against constitutional rights.

This rite is one of the ones about which you will not want to notify the press. This is especially so if your battle winds up in the courtroom. We are going to be calling on Thoth, and although you and I know that he isn't interested in fixing a court case, the press will probably claim that you are trying to use witchcraft against a judge. We are really attempting to cause the patterns of Thoth to appear in ourselves. To that end, we are calling on a keeper of justice and truth. Thus, only use such a rite if you are absolutely sure it is the truth that you want justice to serve. For if it is not, disastrous results may follow. Do write any applicable letters and do incorporate them into the ritual. Call the press to a press meeting and commemorate the mailing of the letters, but mention absolutely nothing which might be taken as a threat on the impartiality of any legal matter.

Stoke your thurbles with Thoth's incense; anoint your bodies with his oil and your altars with his minerals. If you have jewelry that contains opal and particularly fire opal, place it in the center of the ritual and charge it as you charge the letters. In all matters dealing with this situation, wear both the charged jewelry as well as the Thoth oil.

"All be truth
Thoth, Thoth
All be known
Thoth Thoth
All be just
Thoth Thoth."

As you chant, see a world where it is impossible to lie about either intent or action.

To turn back plague

It might be missing from common knowledge, but the plague that ravaged most of Europe was considered God's wrath by the Church state. The healers of the time were often thought to be in league with the devil because they fought the ravages of their God's divine vengeance. Such ridiculous claims are made time and time about our current plague, AIDS.

The zealots were wrong about the bubonic plague. It was not started by God in his outrage of what men were doing; it was started by karma in its rage against what the Church had done. Countless numbers died because the Church was not willing to open its eyes and observe the simple fact that the only places the plague could be found were those places where the cat population was low and the rat population was high. We should not be surprised that the Church did not notice this correlation because to do so, the Church would have had to recognize that its war on healers and their other imaginary enemies brought them to kill cats on sight. It was strongly believed that cats were the messengers who helped communication between Witches and Satan.

Things haven't changed much. Our cats are no longer considered Satan's messengers, but zealots are still persecuting the victims of plague (AIDS and HIV). Illness is still considered the wrath of God, especially when it strikes someone the Church does not like. The victims of plague are still persecuted for the divine wrath that they have called down. What the zealots are really doing is attempting to justify their own meager existence by blaming someone else. It is kin to Hitler's insistence that Germany was not prosperous because the Jews were holding all the wealth.

Healing these injustices and the plague itself is not a simple case of solitary meditation because, although your intent may be that AIDS victims are treated with respect and dignity, it is the intent of others that they be spat on and rounded up in concentration camps. This challenge is so great, that we must call on multiple forces to hear our plea.

"WooooooooooooooTaaaaaaaaaaaaaaan! Hear our cry!
Our brothers and sisters are about to die!
Their lives have been short and their battles few
All in all they are nothing like you of you
But what, if anything, would you have become
If at your birth the Fenris wolf had won?
WooooooooooooooTaaaaaaaaaaaaaaan! Hear our cry!"

The problem with demons like AIDS is that they are both huge and tiny. Warrior spirit cannot crush what it cannot see. This brings our battle to a different field. There is only one thing that will cure AIDS, HIV, MD, MS, and all the other nasty combinations of letters. There is only one thing that will defeat the cancer that took my father's life, and there is only one thing that will rid this world of the other microscopic demons that consume the body one cell at a time. That one thing is money.

The warrior spirit may not be able to combat the micro-organisms of this battle, but it can be used to raise awareness and crush the popular pagan idea that money does not matter. To believe that it does not is not a Wiccan archetype of our protector and provider, and it should not be an archetype of our community.

Be it disease, poverty, cruelty to animals, or any other value that our community claims, using real magick to cause real external change is a noble cause. It should fill our hearts, minds, and our festivals. This is how the real pre-Christian pagan conducted himself, and this is how the real neopagan should conduct himself. Anything else and you are just amusing yourself with role-playing games.

Think global! Act local!

Chapter 6

To Cause Etheric Change

In terms of physics, ether is a theoretical medium that conducts electromagnetic radiation. This conductor was once believed to fill all unoccupied space. This theory is a way of describing the principle of absolute motion. It includes the belief that there are physical coordinates in existence that are universally the same from everyone's viewpoint.

In terms of magick, ether is the substance by which all things are created. It is also called spirit and Akasha. The top point of the Wiccan pentagram represents ether because it is said to triumph over the physical elements. In Wiccan ritual, ether is the force that brings Air (masculine) to Earth (feminine), Fire (masculine) to Water (feminine), and Lord to Lady.

The ether is most often described as residing in the place beyond the vails. It is where those who have left this world reside until their reincarnation. It is where Summerland can be found. It is where the Akashic records are kept and it is where divine knowledge comes from. It is the source of miracles and inspiration. It is Mount Olympus. It is where all god forms reside. In some rather stuffy and overly dramatic lore, it has been called the shadow realm. It is the place that demons come from.

We do not need such shadows. Our magick and our demons come from within. According to the etheric theory, all motion is absolute because it passes through a specific amount of ether. Because light maintains a constant speed, light will pass through any specific amount of ether in the same amount of time, regardless of the vantage point to the event. This scientific theory falls apart when you toss in vantage points and their relationship to movement.

If you were able to place a beam of light in between two perfect mirrors and bounce that light back and forth in a vertical direction, it would appear to you to be traveling at the speed of light. That doesn't sound very hard to believe. Light travels at the speed of light.

Now what happens if you get into a moving vehicle with that beam of light bouncing back and forth? From your perspective, the light appears to continue to travel at the speed of light. But from the perspective of someone who is not in that vehicle, the light is not only traveling vertically. The horizontal movement of the vehicle causes the beam of light to appear to be moving diagonally from the vantage point of someone standing still. From the vantage point of the person outside the vehicle, the beam of light is covering more distance by moving diagonally than from the vantage point of the person inside the vehicle, who observes the beam of light to move horizontally.

If you are having trouble with this image, think of a tennis ball bouncing between the roof and floor of your car. Let's consider one bounce of the ball that starts on the floor and then hits the roof. If that ball appears to travel in a straight line from the floor to the roof to anyone inside the car, it will appear to travel diagonally to anyone standing still outside the car. This is because you are traveling with the car. From your vantage point, the ball has just traveled from the floor to the ceiling. From the vantage point of someone who is not traveling with the car, the ball started on the floor where the floor started, and ended on the ceiling where the ceiling ended. As both the floor and the ceiling are moving with the car, the starting bounce was behind you by the time the finishing bounce strikes the ceiling. Thus the ball travels horizontally with the movement of the car and vertically with its bounce.

The scientific theory of ether explains the movement of the tennis ball easily. The diagonal movement was the correct assessment because the tennis ball traveled a very specific distance through the substance of ether. If the person sitting in the car were to measure that quantity of ether that the tennis ball passed through, he would come up with the same measurement as the person observing the event.

The theory would be fine if everything moved with the same laws as the tennis ball, but everything does not move under the same laws. Light has a special little law of its own. Light must travel at the speed of light (unless hindered). It cannot slow down. What this means is that it cannot possibly pass a different amount of space in the same amount of time.

Science muddled around with the dilemma for some time. Then came a man I like to call "Uncle Al." He was probably the greatest magician to ever walk the Earth. Of course, some readers will assume I am speaking of Aleister Crowley. But I am referring to a man who puts Crowley to shame, even though he had trouble lacing his own shoes.

Albert Einstein questioned the scientific law of ether. He knew that natural law says that the speed of light is a constant. It cannot change with movement. Thus, something else had to be changing when light travels a greater distance when observed from a stationary point. Something else does change the perception of those who are observing the event. If the light that is bouncing between those hypothetical mirrors appears to travel twice the distance from a stationary position, then it will appear to take twice as long to travel that distance. The rate at which time passes for the people who are stationary will appear to speed up to the person who is in the vehicle and vice versa.

This theory has been tested by placing precision time keeping pieces in a train and at a stationary post. Time and time again, the two timepieces were compared after lengthy trips and invariably the one that was on the train appeared to slow down during the journey. In the extreme, this means that if you were to travel for one year at approximately the speed of light, anyone who you left behind would experience approximately two years of life. The ratio is established because by doing so, the x and y axis of a diagonally traveling beam of light viewed from a stationary position would be twice as long as the vertical access viewed from within the space ship.

Uncle Al's theory became widely known as the theory of relativity. Recent movies and other fiction have advanced the idea that although natural laws cannot be broken, they can be bent. This concept is not an accurate depiction. Natural law is impermeable. What you can change is your level of understanding of natural law. Uncle Al did not break a natural law when he shattered the theory of ether. He simply demonstrated that ether is not a natural law, but relativity is. It is time for our magickal model of the universe to catch up with the scientific view of a man who died in 1955.

I love every memory that I have of my father. My brother does not share this love and my mother's opinion is somewhere in between. I believe with all my heart that my father was a sincerely good man. My brother believes my father was an abusive drunk. My mother thinks my father was a good man who had a few faults.

Under the theory of ether, it is not possible for all three of us to be correct. But under the theory of relativity, it is not only possible that our differing views are each true, it is impossible for us to have completely same views. Consider one of the other assertions Uncle Al included with his theory of relativity: "...events that appear simultaneous to an observer in one system may not appear simultaneous to an observer in another system" (from *The Concise Columbia Electronic Encyclopedia, Third Edition*).

The "system" that we use to "observe" history is memory. We do not have to leave our bodies to enter what magicians refer to as the etheric universe, because that universe is within our own mind. There is absolutely nothing supernatural about it. I have a much higher opinion of my father because I entered the etheric universe and changed my history by changing the key memories of my father. Nothing has been repressed and nothing has been altered except where I place my focus. Although my memories differ greatly from those of my brother, neither one of us has a more correct record of my father's life because each record is relative to the individual.

Because the etheric world is really part of this world, we can make changes to that world just as easily as we can make changes to this world. Techniques for doing so have been a part of just about every culture that has sought to better itself.

Dreaming

The mysteries of the universe are hidden in plain sight. Almost all of us have watched a scary movie before bed only to wake with a bad dream. Those of us who have worked very repetitive jobs have awakened to the realization that our workplace has invaded our dream state. Dreams follow us into our waking moments as well. Who hasn't seen events in the real world unfold in the same order as in a dream?

When we question the events surrounding our dreams, it becomes very obvious that our dream world and our waking world are not the separate things that we have been told. The dream world is just more fluid than the waking world because it has not been assigned solid form. The interaction between the dream world and what we perceive as the real world allows us to use one to change the other.

To encourage pleasant dreams

Place amethyst and citrine crystals in a blue sachet with lavender flowers. Put the sachet into your pillowcase. The amethyst encourages good dreams and the citrine discourages nightmares. If you want to encourage sexual dreams, include sunstone. If you want to encourage the same in a female mate, include moonstone. Place a few drops of dream or lavender oil on the sachet and one drop on each temple.

To remember your dreams

Keep a tape recorder next to your bed. If you don't snore, try a voice-activated model. The moment you wake, record everything you remember. Don't worry if it does not make sense as you speak it. When you listen to the tape in a waking state, there will be plenty of time to analyze it.

To dream of a specific person

Your dreams are not limited in space and time, so don't limit your intentional dreaming to either. This technique is most often useful in our dealings with loved ones who have crossed. Place a picture of him or her under your pillow. If you want to focus on positive memories, pick a photograph taken at a positive event. If you want to confront a negative memory, pick a photograph taken at that negative event. If you do not have photographs or if you want to augment the photographs, write a journal of everything you remember about a person in a three-ring binder. Select chapters that you want to explore in your dreams, remove them from the binder, and read them before going to sleep.

To tune the environment to a specific person, diffuse their astrological oil, burn their incense, prepare their favorite meals, and leave a portion out for them to share. Arrange the furniture of your home in the way that they did (or would have). If you have a particular outfit that they were fond of seeing you wear, wear it to bed.

Sharing simultaneous dreams with others

Dreamtime and indeed the whole of consciousness is a shared reality. When in dream state, we interact with others in the same way we interact in the waking portion of our world. The reason we do not readily recognize this is because these interactions are based on proximity. In the waking state, we see this proximity as being related to physical location. In the dream state, this proximity is based on the perceptual location. This is why we tend to meet the same individuals in our dream state repeatedly, the same way we tend to experience the same individuals in our waking state again and again.

The way to bridge these two seemingly separate worlds is to cause similarities to occur in each. If you want to share a dream with another person from your waking world, spend time with her. A direct connection to another person can more easily be made in the dream world when we have direct connections to that person in the waking world. Shared experiences in one tend to lead to shared experiences in the other. Spend the day prior to your shared dream attempt doing the same things, eating the same foods, and listening to the same music. Anoint the temples with dream oil of the same ingredients. Even if your experiment should fail, compare your dreams and try again while focusing on those things that your dreams had in common.

Dreaming your success

Dreams and creative visualization are virtually the same thing. Each tends to occur with or without our intent, and both tend to manifest in what we generally perceive as the more tangible world. You can direct your dreaming mind in the same way you direct your waking mind. Remember that scary movie that invaded your dream world? Chances are, it was the last thing you were thinking about when you drifted off. Harness this power by controlling what is on your mind when you fall asleep.

Dreaming a promotion at work

Identify the qualities and events that will assure your promotion. Place success oil on both temples and concentrate with intent on having those qualities and partaking of those events. It is sometimes necessary for management to observe these qualities and events. Use the techniques listed with 'To dream of a specific person' to bring your boss or management into your dream and show them why you deserve the promotion. With your thoughts focused, it is likely that those thoughts will continue into the dream state. With those thoughts manifest in the dream sate, it is likely they will manifest in the waking world.

Dreaming a perfect lover into your life

If you can meet the woman of your dreams in your dream world, you can meet her in your waking world. The problem with such operations is that when most people think about meeting the woman of their dreams, they think about the manifestation of that woman. If you start with the already manifested, you will tend to use that manifestation to backward engineer your intent. That will lead to disaster.

Instead, try to find your dream lover based on your intent. Hopefully, that intent will exclude such shallow attributes as race, height, weight, and other physical characteristics, but if you want to limit your desire go right ahead; after all, it is your mental well-being that is at hand. Use the previously listed techniques, but instead of using props that will directly link to a person, try to find things that will link to the attributes of the person you are looking for. If you want a woman who likes animals, use pictures of animals under your pillow and try to find your dream lover in parts of the ether that include animals. If you desire a woman who has an interest in poetry, read poetry before sleeping with your poetry journal under your pillow.

As anyone who has ever had a monotone professor can tell you, one does not have to be sleeping to achieve dream state. When we do this unintentionally, it is called daydreaming. When done deliberately, it is sometimes called astral projection. Be it dreaming, daydreaming, or astral projection, each is an act of entering what we call the ether.

Waking interactions with the dead

Lore tells us that contact with those who have left this world is most likely to occur on Samhain, the night when the veils between worlds is at its thinnest. Indeed, I have had the best success with large groups in that general season. Each year for some time, we have held a public celebration called the Real Witches Ball. I cannot remember a time when someone who attended main ritual did not fall to his knees overcome with tears because he had made contact with a loved one that had passed. With main ritual attendance in the hundreds, one might think our ritual team was highly trained in such matters. The truth is, absolutely nothing ever goes as planned. Nonetheless, it still works because everyone who is in attendance brings her past loved ones with her. We do not convince our guests' ancestors and loved ones to enter our circle; our guests do because they have no choice. Each and every one of us has a permanent connection to every one we have ever loved.

The hardest part about making contact is finding a time and place to be alone and uninterrupted. You will need two candles, a very comfortable chair, a room that can be completely darkened, and a large mirror. You will also need mugwort, lavender, sandalwood, and the ability to burn natural incense. I prefer freestanding oval mirrors. Be aware that you will probably lose all track of time, so unplug the telephone and plan on staying up late.

Wash the mirror with an infusion of mugwort and place an incense burner stoked with charcoal. Light the coals in a different room and bring them into the room only once they have stopped sparking. The sulfur that is in many self-lighting charcoals is a banishing agent. The same is true of the candles if you are lighting them with a match. Arrange your furniture such that the chair is close enough to the mirror that the mirror takes up at least one half of your horizontal range of sight. Place the candles behind you and to the left and right at about a foot below eye level. You should not be able to see the candles' direct reflection in the mirror, but they should slightly illuminate the smoke that will rise from the incense burner.

Concentrate on your most recent memory of a conversation with the person you wish to contact. As you do, toss some of the lavender onto the coals, then some sandalwood. Try to generate just enough smoke that it is noticeable in the darkness, but not so much that the mirror will be obscured.

Try to focus just beyond the surface of the mirror. See it as having depth, like a pool of water. Focus your eyes on the fish that swim beneath the surface of that water. Continue to focus your mind on your most recent memory of a conversation with the person you wish to contact. If that person is willing and able, he will interact with you through the visual aid that you have used to create a portal to your mind.

Achieving this interaction is easy. Understanding the language in which you can exchange information is not. When your session is over, write down every impression you received during your efforts. Meaning may not instantly associate itself with everything that you observed; sometimes it takes a while before the messages take on clear meaning. Do not despair; this method seems to work for just about everyone.

Astral travel

This is probably the single hokiest-sounding topic you will find in this book. It is also one of the ones that seems to work with just about everyone. With its reference to the "astral plane," the concept of travel is difficult to understand. The key is that you are not leaving your body at all. As with dreaming, astral projection is an exploration of your mind and the interconnections it has to the total human experience.

This is why the ability to travel the astral plane during sleep seems inherent to most humans. The dream state is a place in which our sensory input is limited. Without external distractions, it becomes easier to focus on that which is internal. Often times we wake with knowledge we could not have gathered by any other methods. With practice and training, some amazing results have been achieved in both the waking and sleeping states. This ability is so attractive that the governments of the United States and the former Soviet Union have spent considerable time, money, and other resources to research its military applications. In those applications, the process was called remote viewing.

The Shamanic Technique of astral projection: Throw yourself at the ground and miss

There are many techniques for achieving astral travel. I have had my best results with what can be described as the Shamanic method. I call this the Shamanic technique because it incorporates Shamanic customs more than other techniques; thus it is important to note that practicing this rite no more makes one a Shaman than changing a tire makes one a mechanic.

Eliminate the potential of distraction. Go skyclad if you are comfortable with it. Wear loose-fitting clothing if you are not. Never eat directly before attempting astral travel or put off eating prior to your efforts. Ideally, you will be neither hungry nor bloated.

Although sensory depravation is a common prerequisite for astral travel, entering the altered state in which travel is achieved can be assisted by our senses. The steady beat of a drum (use a CD if it is really necessary), chant, or rattle is often used in the Shamanic technique. Having a partner is just about mandated for this technique. A small group of trusted friends is much better. In tribal culture, the information that was retrieved from such travels was used to benefit the entire tribe. It is very possible that you will acquire knowledge that will help the friends who assist you, so don't feel that asking for their assistance is selfish.

Although you may well achieve a completely different goal, each journey should have a specific intent. With that intent in mind, choose a god form to guide you. Chapter 9 contains a brief list of god forms to help you decide. Anoint your body with his oils, eat his favored foods, burn his incense, and explore his lore. Get to know your guide in every way you can prior to your journey.

Cast your circle as you would normally. For smudging, burn a mixture of lavender and sage. If you can, work with the energy flow of your chakras to strengthen your aura. When it is time to invite the Lord and Lady, call on the god form that you have chosen as your guide. If you are working with a group in which others will attempt the process, let the invitation be spoken in a generic fashion but speak his name internally. Although it is your mind that you are entering, the visualization of your aura will be what you take with you as what is called the astral body. Begin the drumming or other sources of rhythmic noise, and start your favorite chant.

In a clockwise direction, move about the ritual area in a circle. Move with the beat of the drum in the manner of your heart. The drummers and chanters should understand that the beat should increase slowly as you circle. The goal is for the beat to reach frenzy right about the time of your exhaustion. After at least three trips around the circle, you will find your state of mind changing. Some of this is due to the toxins that build in your blood; it is normal with any physical activity. At the point where you feel you just cannot continue, you will have hit what is commonly called the runner's wall.

See that wall as the ground in the center of your circle. With the last portions of energy, fall to that wall. As you do, see the momentum of your dance travel with you towards the Earth. See your guide riding that momentum with you. At the moment of impact, feel your aura (astral body) punch a hole through that wall at its strongest point (the head) bringing with the full momentum of your dance and all that it has swept up (yourself and your guide). Feel your mind open as if it were a tunnel into which the momentum of your dance has forced your guide and yourself to spiral into. At this point the drumming should slow and soften to the rate of a heart at rest.

To achieve astral projection with meditation (for those who can't dance)

If colliding with the Earth is not your idea of an Earth-based religion, the meditative technique is another option. It is also an option if you find yourself too distracted by noise to achieve travel with the background of a drumbeat. I should note that I have had much less success with this technique.

Cast a circle in the normal way except that when you smudge, do so with astral projection incense. When it comes time to invite the Lord and Lady, use a god form that corresponds with the intent of your travel.

Place a few drops of astral travel oil or tincture on each temple. The exact circumstances in which one can achieve astral travel will change from individual to individual. If the presented formula for oil and tincture does not work for you, see Chapter 9 for other associations that might. The same is true of the incense that is used to smudge the circle.

Better yet, have your lover massage your temples lightly with the oil while you attempt to extend yourself outside of your body. Tumbled quartz seems to aid astral travel greatly, especially when tourmalated. If you have access to these, rub them on your temples and then place them on your forehead (if lying down) or crown (if sitting).

Achieving deliberate astral travel is sometimes elusive in a waking state. Allow yourself to drift into slumber during attempts until you can induce travel easily by that method. If you have a willing partner, have her do this until you drift off to sleep (be willing to exchange the favor). You will be absolutely amazed at the dreams you can achieve. Do not speak the chant yourself, but if you are using a partner ask her to repeat the words as you drift off:

> "Dream the travel
> Dream the flight
> Dream the trip
> It starts tonight."

After you have become proficient while using the sleep state, practice with the intent to travel during waking moments.

Whichever method you use, be ready for many failures before and after you become successful. Even those few folk who take to astral travel like fish to water will tell you that sometimes they simply cannot achieve the state that is necessary to enter the astral plane. Pay close attention to your activity during the week prior to the attempt. Record what you eat and drink. Look for correlations between seemingly unrelated factors and your success or failure. Simple things such as the protein level in your diet seem to make a very large difference. I was not able to achieve astral projection until I became a very strict vegetarian. With the tremendous variety of activities and diets, there is no way to predict what might inhibit any one person. However, once you become proficient at achieving an astral state with these rituals, it will become easier to achieve the same results without such time-consuming preparations.

Remote viewing

Once you have achieved an astral state, focus anyplace with which you are greatly familiar. Your home is ideal, but anyplace on which your memory will assist your observation will do. Notice more details than where the furniture is. Try to note where your favorite coffee cup is, what is the date on the newspapers, where your partner left a magazine. If you are practicing alone, toss a deck of playing cards into a room prior to attempting a projection. Then visit that room in the astral and notice which cards were face up. Once you can reliably bring back information from a familiar location, attempt unfamiliar locations and see if you can accomplish the similar results.

This is possible because, like the more tangible plane, the astral plane is a shared reality. In a non-astral state, it is not necessary to have a memory of a place that does not yet appear to reside in your mind. Even if someone else built a house, you can enter and move about. The astral plane is no different except that physical travel does not take place. If the thought of that house exists in a person's mind, that house exists in the astral.

The greatest potential in astral travel can be found in its offer of knowledge. Virtually every potentiality exists scattered around different parts of the astral. If there is a cure for AIDS, it rests in bits and pieces that need only be assembled. The downside to recovering such information is that, just like in the real world, most of us could hold such a cure in our hands and have absolutely no idea what it was. So go with what you know. Artists can improve their artwork by viewing the potentiality of other artwork. Computer programmers can improve their programs by viewing the potentiality of other computer programs. The upside is that international copyright laws have not yet reached this plane. Besides, the astral contains concepts not concrete. In computer terms, the astral is strictly open source.

Healing the past

No one was born to a perfect family. None of us has enjoyed a perfect life during every moment that preceded this one. Our past is filled with events that may hold us back and haunt us from time to time. Although these demons are very real, we can sometimes be tricked into thinking there is nothing we can do about them because they exist in the past. If that were the case, then there would be nothing they could do to us as well. Influence is a two-way street. If the past can influence you, you can influence the past.

Key memories can be changed. If you were beaten by someone you also shared good times with, focus your thoughts on the memories of the good times. Make two dolls to represent the duality of your feelings for that person. If you can, use the person's clothing. Look up the herbs that correspond to that person's zodiac sign (see Chapter 9). Pick as many of the edible herbs as you can and taste them. Stuff the doll that represents the bad memories with the herbs that tasted bad; stuff the good with the good-tasting herbs. Personalize the dolls with their good qualities and with their bad qualities.

If the negative memory involved alcohol, put a bottle in the bad doll's hand. Miniature bottles are available at just about every craft store. If a positive memory involved baking cookies, put a cookie in the good doll's hand. Be creative and do what you can to make the dolls not only represent the person, but the duality of your feelings about that person.

Talk to the dolls and explain why you had to separate them. Let the bad doll know that he can continue to be a part of your life only if he doesn't present you with further problems. Should you encounter further problems with the memories, place the bad doll in a box and explain why you are locking him away. If he acts up again, bind him with duct tape. If you encounter one last bout, toss him in a moving body of water. Feel the connection between him and you drift away or sink to the bottom.

If you have photographs that represent a bad memory, place them in a mason jar. Fill the mason jar halfway with heavily salted water. Heat this in a double boiler and seal it when it is hot. Tie a black ribbon around the neck of the bottle three times and anoint with banishing oil. Place it in the back of the freezer next to the turkey leg you forgot from last year's holiday dinner. If this doesn't put the memory in the furthest reaches of my mind, I have been known to take the jar to my local shooting range and blast it a few times with a 12-gauge. Sure, the glass shatters and for an instant the visual affect is that the memory was released, but your mind doesn't process information quick enough to notice. Instead, it sees the representation of that memory all but disintegrate.

Magick and Spellcraft in Lore

W henever you make or spend time working with a preparation, meditate on the intent. If you are grinding herbs, don't cheat by using your coffee grinder. Use a mortar and pestle. As you do, hold the pestle (masculine) in your projective/dominant hand and the mortar (feminine) in your receptive/submissive hand. Visualize the two genders joining to create the child that is your intent. If you are blending oils, shaking tinctures, or mixing powders, always concentrate on the specific intent of that preparation at each step of the way.

Absolutely do not make or purchase a preparation for future use. This will be particularly tempting with tinctures as they take a couple of weeks to prepare. A large amount of the spell is the meditation that creating the preparation will cause. Even if your only preparation is to get in your car and drive to the store, do so with specific intent.

Give away anything left over from a nonspecific preparation. If the preparation was for general wealth or good fortune, then give it to someone who you know will not make their own preparations. This way at least they will be using something you know was made with heart. Throw away anything left over from a preparation for a specific intent. If you preparation was to help you get a specific job, bury it, drop it in a river, scatter it to the woods, but do not let any other person use that preparation. This will force you to acquire new materials for each new intent. This does not mean you should throw out that new bag of herb or bottle of essential oil. But if you made incense, oil, tincture, or another preparation with intent, get rid of it after the spell is finished.

Chapter 7

Magickal Incense and Tinctures

Stick and cone incense are not the best for use in spellcraft because neither allows the control that natural powders do. Both stick and cone incense require components that may interfere with the effect we seek. Stick incense is typically formed around a thin piece of bamboo. That might be acceptable if our intent aligned with the properties of bamboo, but even then the harsh smell of burning wood adds a generally unpleasant undertone. Cone incense requires a binding agent that might interfere with our intent.

The alternative and best incense form to use for spellcraft is a combination of powdered incense and charcoal disks. The disks can be found in most New Age and pagan shops in packs of five and 10. The price will vary, but generally speaking, you will pay about $2 for 10 disks. You will learn to make the incense in this chapter.

To use incense with charcoal disks, turn the disk upside down so that the cup faces down. Hold the disk to a flame until it starts to spark, then invert it and place it on a bed of gravel or sand in a censor or other fire-safe container. At first, it will smell similar to lighting a match because both contain sulfur. As sulfur has its own magickal properties, it is a good idea to keep the burning disk away from your ritual area until the initial sparks go out. The sparks will stop after a minute or two. When the disk starts to turn white and glow, you can sprinkle on the incense. Smoke will rise immediately. How long your incense will smolder is dependent on the ratio between plant material and resins. A side benefit to using powder incense is its versatility. Almost any powder incense can also be used to make tinctures.

Tinctures that can be made from these incense recipes can be substituted for the oils listed in Chapter 8. Tinctures are much more affordable than essential oils, but they are generally not available at your local pagan shop because, although most extracts that are used in cooking are themselves tinctures, anyone other than a grocery store will generally be hit with a fine or imprisonment for selling alcohol without a license. After a teenager was suspended for drinking ginseng extract at his school, gas stations and grocery stores were forced to remove boxes of ginseng extract or face the potential of jail time. But that does not mean that it is illegal for you to make your own tinctures. The violation of law only comes in when you try to sell the product without having a liquor sales permit.

The alcohol used to create a tincture is grain alcohol (a.k.a. ethyl alcohol or ethanol). It is the same material that our gasoline has been spiked with for years. But don't try making your tinctures with unleaded fuel or rubbing alcohol (isopropyl). Although both will do a bang-up job of extracting the scent from the plant material, they will also add their own scent.

The absolute best alcohol for this purpose is good old Everclear (192 proof / 96%). I have seen claim after claim that you can use any grain of 140 proof/70%, but I have yet to find vodka in that strength and all of the other alternatives leave an afterscent. Bacardi 151 will do if you absolutely cannot find Everclear, but it comes with its own annoying odor. Better to save the rum for libations and go with the good stuff.

There are devices on the market that will generate top-quality tinctures much faster than what I will describe. But thus far, I have found them all overpriced, and some were downright dangerous. If you must experiment with such devices, avoid any that use an open flame, ignore their instructions on solvents (usually petroleum ether), and be ready for a visit from your local law enforcement agency; these devices are often used to concentrate the THC from marijuana into hashish or hashish oil (sometimes with the assistance of battery acid to rotate the CBN into THC). I hope I just caused a few people to rethink the use of hashish.

Instead, let's use the tried-and-true method. Assemble your dried plant material and grind it to the smallest possible portions. If you are using hard materials such as gallangal or sandalwood, you will be better off purchasing the herb in powder form. Cover the bottom of a standard size mason jar with the plant material. Pour in the alcohol to an amount equal to twice the volume of the plant material. If the plant material is one inch deep, the alcohol should rise one inch above it for a total of two inches in depth. Screw on the cap tightly and then shake.

Unscrew the cap to release the pressure, then tighten and shake the jar vigorously for three minutes. Repeat this at least once; better thrice, a day for half a lunar cycle (two weeks). Always store the jar in a cool place away from direct light of any kind. I have had better success if I do this during the first two weeks of a lunar cycle (new moon to full moon) that corresponds to the intent. After two weeks, enough of the plant material should have fused with the alcohol so that you will be able to detect it in the scent of the tincture. To test this, place a drop or two on your wrist and allow it to evaporate. If there is a distinct odor after the alcohol has evaporated, you have succeeded in creating a successful tincture.

Dry incenses tend to burn entirely too fast. To slow down the burn, I have found that including enough of an oil base to barely dampen the mixture works great. Do not saturate the powdered plant material. Just enough oil is added so that if you pinch the mixture together it will bind to itself. Add too much oil and the mix simply will not burn. With just the smallest amount of practice you will get a feel for how much oil to include. If you are making tinctures, you can skip the binding agent, but it won't hurt if you include it for tincture blends as well.

Where a reference is made to an oil by the same name as the incense or tincture, that oil should be prepared from the instructions given in this book, as they were formulated to complement each other. Failing that amount of preparation, the substitute given can be used, or you can pick a different substitute from Chapter 9, where associated concentrations and extracts are given. The same is true of substituting associated plant materials.

Incense and tinctures of the Gods

Every Wiccan ritual includes an invitation to the Lord and Lady. Many times, this takes the generic form of Father Sky and Mother Earth. This is fine if the ceremony has a generic theme. Thus is the case when you bring together people from many different traditions whose focus might be much separate from your own. Allowing all members of your circle to view the Lord and Lady with their own eyes is always preferable in such situations.

Spellcraft is not one of those situations. When we cast a spell, we do so with very clear (non-generic) intent. Once your intent is clear, pick the archetype associated with that intent. Chapter 9 lists many of my favorite male archetypes and their general associations. This information is limited for obvious reasons. Consider reading *The Witch's God* by Janet and Stewart Farrar. When you are comfortable with your choice of archetype for a particular effort, replace your normal ritual incense with one better suited to favor the attendance of that deity.

Remember also that spellcraft is not always conducted with the formality of ritual. Each of these incenses can be burned, bundled into sachets ("mojo/gris gris bags"), or used in tincture form whenever you wish to strengthen your bonds to these archetypes. These blends are designed not only to honor the god form, but to help you find their pattern within your own psyche.

Adonis Samhain and Adonis Beltane

2 parts myrrh (sweet myrrh if you can find it)
1 part bay leaf
1 part gum arabic
1 part red rose petals or 9 pomegranate seeds (depending on the season)
Enough Adonis or myrrh oil to bind

If you are making and using this mixture between Samhain and Beltane, use the pomegranate seeds. If you are making and using it between Beltane and Samhain, then use the rose petals. Incidentally, with pomegranate seeds, this is an excellent choice of incense for all matters of death, and makes a wonderful general incense choice for Samhain. The same is true of the version with rose petals and Beltane, or celebrations of life's victory over death. The pomegranate seeds represent the cold darkness of death that is necessary to bring the warm light of life. Each is necessary for life to continue.

An offshoot of this recipe is "Life and Death incense/tincture." Instead of choosing between rose petals and pomegranate, combine nine pomegranate seeds with one-half ounce rose petals. Then, add that mixture to an ounce of myrrh or sweet myrrh and a half ounce of both bay and gum arabic.

Aeacus

Burn to assist in decisions of wealth.

3 parts frankincense
3 parts allspice berries
1 part cinnamon
Enough Aeacus or frankincense oil to bind

Agni

Burn to assist in sudden change.

2 parts hibiscus flower
1 part nettle herb
1 part dragon's blood
A pinch of poppy seeds
Enough Agni or dragon's blood perfume oil to bind

Apollo

Burn for added guidance during rites of prophecy, divination, and healing.

1 part acacia
1 part bay leaf
1 part gum arabic
Enough Apollo or cypress oil to bind
(If you are making a tincture, add two dates to this recipe.)

Ares

Military Wiccans can use the smoke of this incense to bless their gear prior to combat.

2 parts dragon's blood
1 part benzoin
1 part nettle
A pinch of wormwood
A pinch of rue
Enough Ares or benzoin oil to bind
A few drops of accidentally spilled blood*

I do not encourage anyone to intentionally draw blood for the purpose of making a magickal preparation. But if you should accidentally cut yourself while doing something else, and happen to have this mixture on hand, by all means capture your blood in this incense or tincture.

Asclepius

Burn in conjunction with any healing rite that involves hands-on healing. This is also an excellent incense to burn while using Reiki.

2 parts juniper berries
1 part bay

1 part arabic gum
Enough Asclepius or juniper berry oil to bind

Bacchus

Burn prior to revelry to heighten the atmosphere to that intent.

2 parts patchouli
1 part thistle
1 part gum arabic
Enough Bacchus oil or a combination of red wine and field honey to
bind.

Brahma

Burn during rites of creation and to promote fertility.

2 parts cedar wood
1 part hyssop
1 part cypress
Enough Brahma or cedar wood oil to bind
(If you are making a tincture, include two dried figs).

Cupid

**Who hasn't tried playing matchmaker? Burning this incense during such
efforts will increase your chances of success. Be warned, such efforts
most often end in disaster.**

2 parts red rose petals and buds
1 part cypress leaf
1 part juniper berries
1 part gum arabic
Enough Cupid, juniper berry, or rose oil to bind

Dionysus

Use as Bacchus incense but a little more refined.

4 parts pine needles
2 parts juniper berries
½ part raisins
Enough Dionysus or patchouli oil to bind

Eros

Use with the same intent as Cupid incense, only do so outside.

4 parts rose petals and buds (see chapter 9 to match color to intent)
2 parts bay leaf
1 part gum arabic
Enough Eros or rose oil to bind (rose oil produces the best scent)

Faunus

Burn this incense to promote the confidence to flirt.

4 parts pine needles
1 part bay leaf
1 part gum arabic
Enough Faunus or pine oil to bind

Ganesa

Burn in conjunction with prosperity rites.

1 part damiana herb
1 part jasmine flower
Enough Ganesa or jasmine absolute to bind

Hades

Burn during rites involving the writing or execution of a person's final will.

2 parts frankincense
1 part hibiscus flowers
1 part poppy flowers
Enough Hades or frankincense oil to bind

Hanuman

Burn during study to promote retention and learning.

2 parts benzoin resin
2 parts sandalwood powder
1 part vervain herb
Enough Hanuman or nutmeg oil to bind

Helios

Burn when taking serious oaths and to seal a magickal promise. This is an excellent incense to burn during hand-fasting rites if one honestly wants the promise to be true.

2 parts frankincense
1 part cinnamon
A few unsalted sunflower seeds
Enough Helios or frankincense oil to bind

Hermes

Wear a sachet of this blend when bringing news to an employer. Also, burn this blend when you need help communicating an idea.

2 parts sandalwood powder
1 part benzoin
1 part gum mastic
Enough Hermes or sandalwood oil to bind

Herne

Burn to commune with the essence of our horned Lord. Also used to heighten male fertility and virility.

2 parts patchouli herb
2 parts pine needles
1 part gum arabic
Enough Herne oil or a mix of patchouli and pine oil to bind

Horus

Burn to fight death and infertility.

2 parts red rose petals and buds
1 part yarrow flowers
1 part dragon's blood resin
Enough Horus or rose oil to bind

Hymen

Burn at hand-fastings to celebrate the union.

2 parts hawthorn betties
2 parts juniper berries
1 part raisins
1 part gum arabic
Enough Hymen oil or red wine to bind the mixture

Indra

Burned prior to combating all types of opposition.

Peel an orange and sprinkle the peel with saffron. Eat the orange and place the sprinkled peel in a warm, moist, and mostly dark place. Spray the orange peel daily with a mixture of warm (not hot) water and the slightest hint of honey. After about a month, you will begin to notice a mold forming on the peel. This mold is the incense or tincture base, not the peel itself.

Only bind this with Indra oil if it is not moist enough to bind by itself.

Jupiter

Burn to promote natural forces to assist growth.

2 parts orange peel powder
1 part cypress
1 part carnation flower
1 part gum arabic
Enough Jupiter or cedar wood oil to bind

(If you are making a tincture from this blend, include one or two figs)

Mars

Use as you would Ares incense.

1 part dragon's blood resin
1 part benzoin
1 part vervain
1 pinch wormwood
Enough Mars or opoponax (sweet myrrh) oil to bind. If using Mars oil, select the type of Mars oil based on the intent of the mixture.

Mercury

Burn to promote communication and for safe travel. Place a white sachet of this mixture in your car or truck to help ward off accidents.

2 parts lavender flower
1 part lemongrass
1 part gum arabic
Enough Mercury or lavender oil to bind.
Best to blend on a Wednesday during either hour of Mercury.

Minos

Burn during the decision-making process when your decisions will affect those who look up to you.

Sandalwood powder dampened with galbanum oil

Odin

Burn during rites similar to those of Ares, but also for rites involving creativity (especially in pottery).

1 part cedar powder
1 part benzoin powder
A pinch of mistletoe
Enough Odin or patchouli oil to bind

Osiris

Burn this incense in your garden when you first plant. It can also be sprinkled there in small quantities.

1 part acacia
1 part benzoin
Enough Osiris or benzoin oil to bind

Pan

Bless your clothes in the smoke of this mixture when looking for a sexual partner, but not when looking for anything more than sex or a sexually active friendship, unless that relationship is intended to be definitely non-monogomous.

1 part pine needles
1 part myrrh
Enough Pan or patchouli oil to bind

Pluto

Burn to assist in judgment, especially in matters of earthly possessions.

1 part hibiscus flowers
1 part poppy flower
1 part frankincense
Enough Pluto or peppermint oil to bind
(If making a tincture, add two figs.)

Poseidon

Sprinkle overboard to assure safe sea travel.

1 part cedar powder
1 part myrrh (sweet myrrh if available)
A pinch of sea salt
Enough Poseidon or myrrh (sweet if available) oil to bind

Priapus

Burn to promote male sexual fertility. This one is very specific in its fertility type; it is for making babies.

1 part myrrh
1 part pine needles
1 part gum arabic
Enough Priapus or pine oil to bind

Set

Burn and sprinkle at boundaries and doors to protect that which is inside.

1 part patchouli
1 part myrrh
Enough Set or patchouli oil to bind

Shiva

Burn to promote acts of destruction which in turn assist creation. A good example would be to sprinkle it in a field that is to be cleared by fire, but not outside of proper fire stops.

2 parts dragon's blood resin
1 part geranium flowers or sandalwood oil dampened with geranium oil
Enough Shiva oil or dragon's blood perfume oil to bind

Shu

Bathe the wand in the smoke of this incense to bless it.

2 parts jasmine
2 parts gum arabic
1 part damiana
Enough Shu oil or jasmine absolute to bind.

Silvanus

Scatter and burn this incense when clearing an area from the woods for rituals. Also a wonderful blend when doing the same for a new home.

1 part pine needles
1 part juniper berries
1 part gum arabic
Enough Silvanus or juniper berry oil to bind

Surya

Burn to help you reach a point of compromise, especially with a wife or lover.

4 parts frankincense
2 parts sandalwood
1 part cinnamon
Enough Surya or sandalwood oil to bind

Thoth

Burn this incense to defeat writer's block and to assist in reaching the wisdom needed to give your words value.

2 parts benzoin
1 part vervain
Enough Thoth or benzoin oil to bind

Zeus

Burn to promote the attributes of a good father.

1 part jasmine flower
1 part hyssop
1 pinch saffron
Enough Zeus or galbanum oil to bind

Incenses and tinctures of the planets

Incenses of the planets are burned with specific intent when attempting to draw on their archetypal patterns as explained in Chapter 9. They are also used to charge talismans that correspond to the specific planetary energy.

Sol (Sun) Oil

2 part cedar powder
1 part copal
1 part benzoin
1 part frankincense
1 part gum arabic
1 pinch saffron
Enough Sol or frankincense oil to bind

Best if made on a Sunday during the hour that falls in between the time of dawn and dusk, or during one of the planetary hours.

Luna (Moon) Oil

4 parts white sandalwood powder
2 parts myrrh (sweet if available)
1 part natural camphor
1 part jasmine flower
Enough Luna or lemon oil to bind

Best if made on a Monday night during the planetary hour or when the moon is full.

Mars

2 parts dragon's blood
1 part allspice berries
Enough Mars, galangal, or ginger oil (best with galangal oil, but true galangal oil is very hard to find)

Best if made on a Tuesday during the planetary hour.

Mercury

2 parts lavender flowers
2 parts lemongrass
1 part gum arabic
1 part benzoin
Enough Mercury, bergamot, or clove oil to bind

Best to blend on a Wednesday during either hour of Mercury.

Jupiter

2 parts cedar powder
1 part juniper berries
Enough Jupiter or pine oil to bind

Best if made on a Thursday, during one of the daylight planetary hours.

Venus

2 parts santal powder (red sandalwood)
1 part red rose petals and buds
1 part lemon peel powder
Enough Venus, rose, or lemon oil to bind

Best if made on a Friday, during one of the nighttime planetary hours.

Saturn

2 parts myrrh
1 part violet
1 part patchouli
Enough Saturn or patchouli oil to bind

Best if made on a Saturday, during one of the planetary hours.

Incenses and tinctures of the astrological signs

Although designed as incense, these combinations work great as the stuffing for dolls that will represent people in your spells. Fill the doll with the mixture associated with that person's zodiac symbol. In spellcraft that calls on you to think of a specific person, either living or dead, burn that person's zodiac incense while attempting to concentrate on the person. This is particularly useful in dream work and healing the past.

You do not have to be focused on a specific person to use these recipes. Find a copy of Linda Goodman's *Sun Signs* and look up the attributes you would like to manifest in an as-yet-undiscovered friend or lover. Determine which sun sign offers the most promise of those attributes. Create two dolls, one filled with the mixture associated with your sun sign and one associated with the sun sign that corresponds to the attributes you seek in a friend or lover. Place these dolls on separate sides of a table. If it is a lover you are trying to attract, put them on a bed. Each day over the course of a month, bring these dolls closer and burn their incenses separately, but closer, each day. On the last day, tie the dolls together in a manner befitting your intent. Friends would most likely be joined at the hand. Burn their incense right next to each other such that the smoke blends together.

Aquarius

2 parts benzoin
1 part lavender flowers
1 part patchouli
Enough Aquarius or cypress oil to bind. Pick the type of Aquarius oil based on the sex of the person this blend is to influence or represent.

Aries

2 parts frankincense
1 part dragon's blood
1 part cloves
Enough Aries or juniper berry oil to bind

Cancer

2 parts sandalwood powder
1 part myrrh (sweet if available)
1 part rose petals (match the color to the intent)
Enough Cancer or palmarosa oil to bind. Pick the type of Cancer oil based on the sex of the person this blend is to influence or represent.

Capricorn

4 parts myrrh
2 parts patchouli
1 part cypress
Enough Capricorn or patchouli oil to bind.

Leo

2 parts sandalwood powder
1 part frankincense
1 part orange peel powder
Enough Leo or cinnamon oil to bind. Pick the type of Leo oil based on the sex of the person this blend is to influence or represent.

Libra

1 part chamomile flowers
1 part rose petals (select color by intent)
1 part gum arabic
Enough Libra or chamomile oil to bind. Pick the type of Libra oil based on the sex of the person this blend is to influence or represent.

Pisces

2 parts sandalwood powder
1 part natural camphor
1 part lemon peel
1 part myrrh (sweet if available)
Enough Pisces or cardamom seed oil to bind

Sagittarius

1 part juniper berry
1 part dragon's blood
1 part frankincense
1 part orange peel powder
Enough Sagittarius or sweet grass oil to bind

Scorpio

2 parts myrrh (sweet if available)
1 part clove
1 part violet
Enough Scorpio or ginger oil to bind

Taurus

1 part patchouli
1 part rose petals and buds (select color based on intent)
1 part gum arabic
Enough Taurus or cardamom seed oil to bind

Virgo

2 parts lavender flowers
1 part lemon balm
1 part gum arabic
Enough Virgo or lavender oil to bind.

Incenses and tinctures of the elements

Elemental incenses are most often burned at the Quarter stones or altars in Wiccan ritual to invite that element (or Watchtower) to watch over the rite. When charging tools, pass those tools through the smoke of corresponding elemental incense.

Earth

Burn to charge and consecrate the ritual pentacle and all symbols of the Earth. Bathe the tool in its smoke.

2 parts patchouli
1 part cypress
Enough Earth or bergamot oil to bind

Air

Burn to charge and consecrate the wand, censor, and other symbols associated with Air. Some traditions stipulate that this will be the incense of choice for the athame, but more and more, the athame is becoming associated with Fire. Bathe the tool in its smoke.

2 parts lavender
1 part benzoin
Enough Air or lavender oil to bind

Fire

Burn to charge and concentrate the athame and all symbols associated with Fire. Bathe the tool in its smoke.

2 parts cinnamon
1 part dragon's blood
1 part frankincense
Enough Fire or allspice berry oil to bind

Water

Burn to charge and consecrate the chalice, cauldron, and all symbols associated with Water. Bathe the tool in its smoke.

2 parts jasmine
1 part lemon peel powder
1 part natural camphor
Enough Water or lemon oil to bind

Incenses and tinctures of the chakras and primary colors

The chakra incenses are used when working with key parts of the body and the energy patterns that are associated with that part of the body. If you are preparing these mixtures for use as tinctures, ordinary food coloring can be used to match the tinctures' appearance to its intent.

These incenses are also very effective ways to promote the emotions associated with individual colors and their corresponding chakra. If you wanted to set the mood for a lustful romantic evening, burn the Red/Root Chakra blend during dinner. Be warned that there isn't a great deal of distance between lust and anger. Burn this one too long and it is sure to become an annoyance. For additional associations, see Chapter 9.

Red/Root Chakra

2 parts patchouli
2 part frankincense
1 part myrrh
Enough Red/Root Chakra or patchouli oil to bind

Orange/Sacral Chakra

2 parts sandalwood
1 part red rose petals and buds
Enough Orange/Sacral Chakra or jasmine absolute to bind

Yellow/Solar Plexus Chakra

2 parts lemon peel powder
1 part sage
Enough Yellow/Solar Plexus or neroli oil to bind

Green/Heart Chakra

2 parts orange peel powder (preferably from unripe oranges)
1 part rose petals and buds
Enough Green/Heart Chakra or bergamot oil bind

Blue/Throat Chakra

3 parts chamomile
1 part natural camphor
Enough Blue/Throat Chakra or neroli oil to bind

Indigo/Third Eye Chakra

2 parts lavender flowers
1 part rosemary leaves
Enough Indigo/Third Eye Chakra or lavender oil to bind

Violet/Crown Chakra

1 part lavender flowers
1 part sandalwood powder
1 part frankincense
Enough Violet/Crown Chakra or lavender oil to bind

Incenses and tinctures of intent

These are just as their stated intent implies.

Astral Travel

Burn when attempting to enter the astral plane.

4 parts lavender flowers
2 parts sandalwood powder
1 part cinnamon
Enough Astral travel or benzoin oil to bind

Banishing

Burn to drive out negative energy.

1 part clove (use asafetida instead, but only if you are truly brave)
1 part frankincense
1 part dragon's blood
Enough Banishing or juniper berry oil to bind

Business Success

Burn outdoors to attract customers and indoors to increase their spending.

2 parts patchouli
1 part clove
1 part cinnamon
1 part basil
1 part benzoin
Enough Business Success oil or patchouli oil to bind. Using a bit of extra patchouli oil is a good idea with this blend, but not so much that it will not burn.

Celibacy Blend for Men

Burn in the morning when you wish to remain celibate through the day. More often than not, this blend is useful when you are away from your lover and do not want sexual urges to distract you from the project at hand.

3 parts lavender
1 part natural camphor
Enough Celibacy or lavender oil to bind.

Courage

Burn in rites designed to bring on courage. Bathe in its smoke prior to situations where you need the extra fortitude to hold your ground in the face of fear.

1 part clove or allspice berries
1 part cedar powder
1 part dragon's blood
1 part frankincense
Enough Courage or ginger oil to bind

Divination

Burn while using tarot cards and other forms of divination. This is a good blend to use to consecrate and charge your divinatory tools.

1 part natural camphor
1 part clove
1 part jasmine
1 part orange peel powder
Enough Divination or orange oil to bind

Dream Blend

Burn prior to sleep to promote dreams.

2 parts lavender
1 part sage
Enough Dream or lavender oil to bind

Energy (physical)

Burn to promote a sense of physical energy. As a tincture, this should be applied to the bottoms of the feet.

2 parts nutmeg
1 part natural camphor
1 part cinnamon
1 part lemon peel powder
Enough Energy or peppermint oil to bind.

Friendship

Burn to promote friendship. If using as a tincture, rub it into your wrists and palms.

1 part lemon peel powder
1 part orange peel powder
1 part gum arabic
Enough Friendship or petitgrain oil to bind

Healing

Burn to promote healing. If using as a tincture, rub it into the area of the body where it is needed, but absolutely do not apply it to any area where there is a physical break in the skin of any kind. This is not intended as a replacement for medical care or common sense.

2 parts sandalwood
1 part allspice berries
1 part rosemary
1 part myrrh (sweet if available)
Enough Healing or juniper berry oil to bind

Joy/Anti-Depression

Burn to drive away the blues and lift the spirit. If using as a tincture, rub it into the chest.

2 parts lemon grass
1 part basil
1 part sage
1 part gum arabic

Enough Joy/Anti-Depression or ylang-ylang oil to bind

Love (for women to feel)

Burn to bring a sense of love in women. If used as a tincture, it should be used as you would massage oil to give your intended target a long foot rub. Warm the tincture gently before using, but do not use open flame.

2 parts gum arabic (if incense) or 4 parts nutmeg (if tincture)
1 part lemon peel powder
1 part peppermint
1 part jasmine
Enough Feminine Love oil or jasmine absolute to bind

Love (for men to feel)

Burn to bring a sense of love in a man. If used as a tincture, it should be rubbed into your thighs and forearms.

2 parts dragon's blood (if incense) or 2 parts lavender (if tincture)
1 part ginger
1 part juniper berry
Enough Masculine Love oil or dragon's blood perfume oil to bind.

Luck

Burn to encourage a sense of luck. If used as a tincture, rub into palms.

2 parts gum arabic (if incense) or nutmeg (if tincture)
1 part orange peel powder
1 part allspice berry
Enough Luck or bergamot oil to bind.

Lust (for women to feel)

Burn to raise lust in the women who smell it. If used as a tincture, use it as you would massage oil, and offer a long deep back rub.

2 parts patchouli
1 part sandalwood
1 part gum arabic (if incense) or 4 parts kava-kava (if tincture)
Enough Feminine Lust or patchouli oil to bind

Lust (for men to feel)

Burn to raise lust in men who smell it. If used as a tincture, rub it into your thighs and abdomen.

2 parts gum arabic (if incense) or yohimbe (if tincture)
2 parts lavender (if incense) or nutmeg (if tincture)
1 part ginger
Enough Masculine Lust or nutmeg oil to bind

Meditation

Burn to help establish a meditative state. If used as a tincture, rub into the area of the neck where the spine meets the skull.

2 parts chamomile
1 part sandalwood
1 part frankincense
Enough Meditation or sandalwood oil to bind

Memory

Burn to bring memories to the surface. Burn while you study and bring memory oil to a test. When you inhale it, the memories of what you studied while burning the incense will return.

2 parts gum arabic (if incense) or clove (if tincture)
1 part rosemary
1 part sage
Enough Memory or juniper berry oil to bind

Prosperity

Burn while working on plans to improve your state of being. If used as a tincture, rub it into each bill that you spend until the prosperity that you seek finds you.

3 parts patchouli
2 parts clove
1 part gum arabic (if incense) or cinnamon (if tincture)
Enough Prosperity or patchouli oil to bind

Protection

Burn for general protection from destructive influences. If used as a tincture, it can be spread at windows and doorways to protect the home.

1 part dragon's blood (if incense) or juniper berries (if tincture)
1 part orris root or a half and half combination of orris root and sage

Purification

Burn for general purification and to remove the outsiders. If used as a tincture, it can be asperged in an area.

2 parts frankincense (if incense) or bay leaf (if tincture)
1 part cinnamon
1 part clove
Enough Purification or benzoin oil to bind

Sexual Energy (for men to feel)

Burn to encourage a sense of sexual vitality in men. If used as a tincture, this should be placed in a bowl to evaporate in the room where a sexual dysfunction or general lack of interest or energy may have occurred.

2 parts dragon's blood
1 part allspice berry
1 part rosemary
Enough Masculine Sexual Energy oil or dragon's blood perfume oil
    to bind

Strength

Burn to bring a feeling of physical strength. If used as a tincture, this should be rubbed into any muscle that you wish to fortify.

2 parts lemongrass (if incense) or 4 parts nutmeg (if tincture)
1 part gum arabic
1 part sandalwood
1 pinch nutmeg
Enough Strength or sandalwood oil to bind

Success and Victory

Burn to bring a sense of success and victory. If used as a tincture, this should be rubbed into the back of your dominant hand.

2 parts gum arabic (if incense) or ginger root (if tincture)
1 part cinnamon
1 part yarrow
1 pinch high john
Enough Success or cinnamon oil to bind

Unstress

Burn to relax and remove stress. If used as a tincture, it should be slowly rubbed into the temples using clockwise patterns.

2 parts lavender flowers
1 part cumin seed
1 part benzoin
Enough Unstress or lavender oil to bind

Wisdom

Burn to promote thought before action. This is also useful to quiet the odd thoughts that enter the mind such that it can focus on one thought. It should not be used as a tincture.

2 parts frankincense
2 parts sandalwood
1 part sage
Enough Wisdom or frankincense oil to bind

Wishing

Burn while making a wish. If used as a tincture, it should be cast to the Earth in front of you as you make a wish. This mixture can also be used to make parchment paper on which to write your wishes. In that case, use sage instead of gum arabic, omit the addition of oil, and follow traditional paper making techniques. The parchment that this produces is ideal for use in the spell listed with wishing oil in Chapter 8.

2 parts sandalwood
1 part gum arabic (if incense) or sage (if tincture)
1 part yarrow
Enough Wishing or sandalwood oil to bind

Magickal Oils

W hen it comes to advice on magickal oils, bookstores seem to offer two distinctly different views. The first type calls the subject aromatherapy. Books in the aromatherapy genre deal almost exclusively with the relationship of oils to human emotions. It is a long-established fact that scent impacts the mind on many levels. The second genre of books on magickal oils are the ones that list such mixtures as money-drawing oil without any attempt at explaining why the oil might help you win at bingo. I believe we can use one of these schools of thought to explain the other.

Most oils that are used in spellcraft are either pure essential oils or a blend of pure essential oils in much more affordable base oil. I have listed a concentration of 21 drops of pure essential oil to one-half ounce of base oil. This is the ratio that I have had the most luck with. It is much stronger than most magickal blends you will find in stores. The reason is twofold. First, essential oils are very costly and shopkeepers want to keep their expenses down. Second, no one wants to wind up in court over a nasty reaction to a strong mixture.

Even if we set aside the fact that the person who will use them best does all magickal preparations, store-bought oils are usually absolute junk. The worst of them are made with the cheapest synthetics available. The best of them are weak; a smoker would be hard-pressed to notice the scent at all. Simpletons are quick to argue that magick works on a quantum level, so even minuscule amounts of true essential oils will work if they are blended in the proper ratio. This idea is ridiculous, as magick is a function of the mind. If your sense of smell is not getting the message to the brain, the oil is useless.

Some blends are deliberately subtle because they are intended to work on a subliminal level. But as a general rule of thumb, if an entire line of oils is weak, then the oil maker is cutting costs. A good test of this principle is to purchase a bottle of Abramelin oil. I have seen the recipe for this oil in a thousand different variants. I have seen it weak and I have seen it strong. However, this oil is the proving ground of anyone who claims to produce authentic magickal oils, as the exact recipe is very easily found in *The Book of the Sacred Magic of Abramelin the Mage,* by S.L. Mathers. Abramelin has such a high concentration of cinnamon and galangal, that it tingles when placed on sensitive skin. The valid argument has been made that Abramelin could not have been speaking about pure essential oils. The extraction methods of his time were not nearly what they are today, but even with the extraction methods of the time, cinnamon and flesh simply do not get along very well.

I have included nothing that is as dangerous as properly prepared Abramelin oil. But you should remember that these blends are just the ones that have worked well for me. You may have more sensitive skin or different reactions than I do, so if you want to be safe, I recommend you use a concentration of one quarter what I have listed until you are absolutely sure the oil will not cause an undesired reaction. Where I have listed most to have a base of one-half ounce, you should start with two ounces and see what the results are. If you are going to use them on your skin, always use them in a very tiny amount at first.

When choosing the essential oils for a mixture, most people research the lore behind the essential oils (scented material). Few people give much thought to the base oil. Most references to base oils are more interested in the oil's longevity than in the properties found in lore. This is unfortunate, as the base oil is typically the largest component of a magickal oil blend. Magickal oils should be used shortly after they are made, so concerns about rancidity should not be an issue. If they are, add three drops of wheat germ oil to each half ounce preparation to help prevent the oils from spoiling.

Base oils

Almond Oil [masculine] (associated god forms: Chandra, Jupiter, Liber Pater, Ptah, Wotan, and Zeus): There are several varieties of almond oil. Look for one with the lightest scent of its own, as strong scents are a sign of artificial additives. It is the oil of choice when the finished product will be used for massage. Because its element is Air, it is an excellent base to use for the consecration and empowering of wands and other tools associated with Air. Lore also tells us that its powers are often used to attract prosperity and wisdom, making it an excellent base for both of these uses.

Apricot Kernel [feminine]: This is rarely seen in magickal formularies, which is sad because I have found it to be the best base oil on which to build love-drawing formulas. Its lore also indicates it to be a good base for projects where you wish to look good, as in courtship or a job interview.

Avocado oil [feminine]: This is a great choice if the oil you are building is designed to inspire lust in either sex. It is also a good base for the ritual anointing (not consecration) of the wand when a female anoints the wand. This is often the case when the full sexual nature of Wiccan rituals is present in symbolic form. The Priest/Host holds the wand as the Priestess/Hostess anoints it.

Coconut Oil [feminine] (Associated god form: Mars): This is an excellent base for oils whose intent is protection or to promote purity. However, it is very thick at room temperature and may have to be warmed to blend. Once it cools, it will become thick and possibly solid again. This is beneficial if the mixture must travel. Because its element is Water, it is an excellent choice for consecration and empowering of chalices and cauldrons. It is also a good base for oils that will be used in conjunction with Water energy and the West Quarter. When we combine the element, gender, and lore, it seems the perfect base on which to build oils to protect pregnant women and newborns.

Grapeseed Oil [feminine] (Associated god forms: Bacchus, Dionysus, Liber Pater): This has very interesting lore. The plant from which it comes is also the plant from which the Greek and Roman pagans made wine. Naturally, there is an association drawn to Dionysus and Bacchus, whose devotees were said to be mostly female. It is also associated with Heather (a fertility goddess), so its associations can be seen as indulgence and fertility. Isn't that always the way?

Hazelnut Oil [masculine]: Considered lucky in its own right, its planetary association is the Sun. It is an excellent base for general good luck and wishing. Like most things derived from nuts, this oil is also considered a good oil for fertility. What? A male oil for fertility? Of course! Nuts and other phallic symbols have long been used in fertility rites and customs. This is an excellent oil on which to base mixtures for Beltane and for the blessings of a Maypole, as well as wands and other phallic symbols.

Jojoba: This is not actually an oil. It is a wax that remains liquid at room temperature. The down side to using jojoba is its price.

The upside is that it will never become rancid, so you do not need to add wheat germ oil as a preservative. Jojoba was used by Native American tribes (especially the Apache) long before European settlers arrived in Northern America. Jojoba originates in the seeds of a shrub (Simmondsia Chinenis), which grows in what is now Southern California. It is interesting to note that prior to its use in the cosmetic industry, its predecessor was oil taken from the sperm whale. Fortunately, jojoba has all of the properties of sperm whale oil (except for the smell), but does not require the senseless slaughter of such a magnificent animal. Because it does not go rancid, it is the perfect base to use when you do not know when the finished product is going to be used. For this reason, it is the only oil I recommend for use in gift or commercial oils. No one wants to receive or purchase an oil to later find it has gone rancid.

Olive Oil [masculine] (Planetary association: sun; Associated god forms: Apollo, Brahma, India, Jupiter, Mars, Poseidon, Wotan): Olive oil is associated with healing and good health. It is also used as the base for home protection, luck, and lust-inspiring oils. With and without being blended with essential oils, olive oil has been used for anointing for a long time.

Palm Oil [masculine]: Brings sexual potency to men and fertility to both sexes. Palm oil is a good base for mixtures designed to protect the home.

Sesame Oil [masculine] (Associated god form: Ganesha): If worn on the body, this is a good oil to base blends to inspire lust. Traditionally used for home prosperity (not for the individual but the household). The classic secret words "open sesame" probably refer to its ability to discover secrets. Use sesame oil as the base for truth and justice oils.

Sunflower Oil [masculine] (Associated god forms: Apollo, Helios, Horus, Surya): This is an excellent base for oils to bring wisdom, wise decisions, and truth. Its element is Fire, making it a good choice for the consecration of tools associated with this element.

While there is some debate as to the elemental association of the athame, I have found sunflower oil to be the best base for consecration of the athame.

Essential oils and absolutes

This is the very essence of scented plant material. Various methods are used to extract the essential oils, including steam distillation and cold pressing. Absolutes are oils that have been obtained using alcohol and fat. Until relatively recently, lard (pig fat) or tallow (beef fat) was used. Today, vegetative fats are generally substituted for the death products. The alcohol and fat method of removing the essential oils is necessary when the scent of the plant is unstable. Most often, this will be with flowers that must be picked during certain weather conditions or times of the day. The plant material is pressed into sheets of fat and left for the fat to absorb the oils from the plant. The oils are then extracted out of the fat using alcohol. The process is much more expensive than either steam distillation or cold pressing, so when you see the word *absolute* next to a choice, check the price before you commit.

There are almost as many potential sources of essential oils as there are plants. Almost, because there are a few plants that simply do not have a fragrant essential oil. If anyone ever tries to sell you "natural strawberry oil," you might want to avoid the merchant in the future. While it may be possible to blend other natural oils to create a scent that smells like strawberry oil, there is no essential oil of strawberry.

Be careful when purchasing essential oils. Unlike the common base oils, true essential oils can be very expensive. As a result, synthetic oils are often marketed in much the same way natural essentials are. Worse yet, some oils that claim to be made with 100 percent natural essential oils actually contain only a portion of the fragrant oil that is boldly listed on the label. If a bottle has the word Patchouli on the label and the phrase "100 percent essential oil," you might be purchasing essential oil of

Patchouli mixed with essential oil of almond (a less expensive fill oil). As each is a true essential oil, the claim is both correct and misleading. The most confusing line of oils are those who sell both true essentials and blends at the same price. To be able to offer a uniform price, the less expensive oils are sometimes sold in pure form and the more expensive oils are diluted in ratio to their expense. I suggest avoiding such products, unless you are going to examine each and every label, then purchase only the true essentials.

When purchasing small quantities, true essentials will most likely come in amber glass bottles. Large quantities often come in special opaque plastic. If your oils arrive in opaque plastic, do not leave them there. Move them to amber glass at a minimum; blue glass is even better. The coloring agents help to prevent the damaging effects of light. Always store oils at a reasonable room temperature away from direct sun light.

Translating formulas for use in candles

It is important to mention that the tinctures in Chapter 7 can be used in place of essential oils in most operations. Making candles is not one of those operations. They may be used for anointing candles, but using highly flammable substances in conjunction with most candle-making operations is incredibly dangerous. The average kitchen contains the fixings of many above-average bombs.

If you want to use these oils to make your own candles, modify the oil recipes by skipping the base oil entirely and translating the number of drops to a ratio of pure essential oils. As an example, lets look at Adonis oil:

9 drops of bay oil translates to three parts
6 drops of myrrh oil translates to two parts
6 drops of rose oil translates to two parts or one part rose geranium and one part cypress oil

When used in candles, any solid material should be ground to an extremely fine powder and never used in a ratio higher than one tablespoon per pound of wax. If using solid plant material, it should always be added to the melted wax first and allowed to blend fully and evenly before the oil is added. Add the oil in a ratio of one and one-half ounce (12 drams) per pound of wax. This is roughly the maximum amount of oil that standard candle wax will hold before it weeps or bleeds oil. You can use a much smaller ratio, but remember that the scent is important, as the scent is what will impact the mind.

Oils of the Gods

These oils are typically used in rites where a particular archetype is called in correspondence with intent. In many Wiccan rites, a candle is lit to represent both our Lord and our Lady. In rites where a specific archetype is being called, anoint that candle with the corresponding oil. The person who will be inviting the lord should anoint his wrists and other body parts where the particular archetype dictates. Such is the case with the temples of horned gods and the ankles of Mercury.

Adonis Oil

Wear this oil to bring heighten masculine beauty.

9 drops bay oil
6 drops myrrh oil
6 drops rose oil* (or 3 drops rose geranium and 3 drops cypress)
1/2 ounce of olive oil

*Note: Okay to use rose geranium if you must to save money, but I have not had as much success drawing on his energy when I make the substitute. I have found myself drawn to reduce the rose by 3 drops and replace it with three drops of cypress oil, but I can find no lore to support the switch other than my own instinct and success.

Aeacus Oil

Anoint a brown candle with this oil and burn to assist in decisions of wealth.

9 drops frankincense oil
9 drops allspice berry oil
3 drops cinnamon oil
1/2 ounce base oil

Agni Oil

This oil is often used to anoint the athame. Anoint a red candle with this oil and burn the candle in conjunction with works to cause sudden change.

9 drops allspice berry oil
6 drops frankincense oil
3 drops cinnamon oil
1/2 ounce base oil

Apollo Oil

Anoint a yellow candle and wear this oil during rites of prophecy, divination, and healing.

12 drops bay oil
6 drops cypress oil
3 drops juniper berry oil
1/2 ounce olive, sunflower, or palm oil

Ares Oil

There are many Wiccans in the military. Although their religion teaches that they should not welcome war, it is sometimes inevitable. In such a situation, anoint each temple and place a drop of protection oil on your flack jacket.

12 drops dragon's blood oil*
9 drops benzoin oil
1/2 ounce olive oil

Dragon's blood oil is a perfume oil, not a true essential.

Asclepius Oil

Rub this oil deep into your hands prior to hands-on healing rites or Reiki.

9 drops bay oil
9 drops juniper oil
1/2 ounce olive oil

Bacchus Oil (Simple)

Ah, if ever a god were missing his horns this would be him. Diffuse this oil where revelry will take place to heighten the atmosphere to that intent.

1/2 ounce patchouli oil
1/2 ounce grapeseed oil
3 drops wheat germ oil
2 drops pine oil
2 drops sweet wine
2 raisins

Add the raisins to the blend and let them bob around in the bottle until you use the oil.

Bacchus Oil (Better)

Following the instructions to make this oil is in and of itself a spell to bring brothers closer together. Sometimes you've got to say, it's time to drink and talk about women. I don't think it's a good idea to bring swords out to the woods on this one, but following these instructions after a game of good-spirited competition is definitely in order. The winner purchases the supplies.

1 part patchouli oil
1 part grapeseed oil
1 part infusion of ivy and thistle
2 tablespoons wheat germ oil
A few raisins
A couple drops pine oil to preference

To make this oil, you will need one other man who won't mind spending an evening in the woods. Bacchus oil should be created while indulging in sweet wine during the full moon of a night that does not precede a work day. It should be blended outdoors.

First, make the infusion by grinding the dried herbs between your hands. Make sure to catch the falling bits on a piece of paper or cloth. Repeat this time and time again until only powder and twigs are left. Then, into a pot of water with the lot of it. That pot should never be larger than one pint. Start a fire under the pot and boil the mixture for a minimum of three hours. Do this while indulging in wine and stories about past, present, and future lovers. Bring a bag of raisins or grapes for supper and toss a few into the boiling pot as you chat. Always spill the first drink of each glass into the pot as an offering and drink fast enough that the pot does not boil away. Do not put out the fire and do not remove the pot. If it goes out on its own so be it, but if the liquid boils away, then you were not meant to have the oil.

Wake after the sun rises. If, and only if, there is cool liquid left in the pot then strain the liquid. One of you adds an equal amount of patchouli oil, the other an equal amount of grapeseed oil. Each adds one tablespoon of wheat germ oil. Pour the concoction into a bottle that will hold it all, cap, and shake wildly. While the mixture is still somewhat blended, pour off one half the mixture into a second jar. Each scent one of the jars to preference with the pine oil, then trade bottles.

Brahma Oil

Anoint the ankles and wrists prior to or during rites of creation or fertility. Also anoint a green candle and burn with similar intent.

12 drops cypress oil
9 drops cedar wood oil
1/2 ounce olive oil

Cupid Oil

If right-handed, anoint the left palm and the index and middle finger of the right hand (reverse when left-handed) when playing matchmaker.

6 drops cypress oil
6 drops rose oil
3 drops juniper oil
1/2 ounce olive oil

Dionysus Oil

Use as Bacchus oil.

9 drops patchouli oil
6 drops juniper oil
3 drops fennel seed oil
3 drops pine oil
1/2 ounce grape seed oil
3 drops red wine
2 raisins

Let the raisins bob in the oil for at least one lunar cycle before using. This oil is similar to Bacchus oil, but much more refined. If you want to use these energies with respect, use Dionysus oil. If you want to get down and really work with a god like this, its Bacchus all the way.

Eros Oil

Used with the same intent as Cupid oil, but to be used on the ankles and wrists.

9 drops bay oil
6 drops yarrow oil
6 drops rose oil (it's expensive but it's worth it)
1/2 ounce olive oil

Faunus Oil

Diffuse and wear on the wrists to reinforce the self-confidence needed to become flirtatious.

9 drops pine oil
9 drops bay oil
3 drops patchouli oil
1/2 ounce olive oil

Ganesa Oil

Anoint your wrists and go to the zoo. There, purchase the food the zoo has for the elephants and feed them while silently asking for Ganesa to help you in matters of prosperity. If your zoo does not have provisions to feed the elephants, do the same but instead of tossing them food, make a donation to the zoo in the name Ganesa.

12 drops jasmine absolute
9 drops damiana tincture
1/4 ounce sesame oil

Hades Oil

Diffuse during rites involving the writing or execution of a person's final will. Adding a drop of this oil to your own will to ensure that it is followed once you have left this world.

12 drops frankincense oil
12 drops hibiscus tincture
6 drops poppy flower tincture
1/4 ounce base oil

Hanuman Oil

Wear on the pulse points to promote your ability to learn.

9 drops sandalwood oil
6 drops benzoin oil
6 drops tincture of mace
1/2 ounce base oil

Helios Oil

Use to anoint the binds used during handfasting rites and the candles of a wedding cake. Goes a long way towards assuring an agreement is honored when that agreement is placed on paper that has been blessed by a drop of this oil.

12 drops frankincense oil
6 drops cinnamon oil
1/4 ounce sunflower base

Hermes Oil

Diffuse during conversations where it is difficult to communicate your thoughts effectively.

9 drops sandalwood oil
6 drops benzoin oil
6 drops gum mastic tincture
1/2 ounce olive oil

Herne Oil

Anoint the inner thigh to heighten male fertility and virility. This is an excellent oil for, uh, well for the bar-hopping approach to finding a female companion who might become a permanent love interest. For quick sex, it is better to use Pan oil.

9 drops patchouli
6 drops pine
6 drops juniper berry oil
1/2 ounce base oil

Horus Oil

Anoint a green candle and burn to combat death and infertility.

9 drops dragon's blood perfume oil
6 drops rose oil
6 drops yarrow oil
1/2 ounce sunflower oil

Hymen Oil

Anoint wedding candles with this oil. Also, anoint a white candle and burn with intent prior to offering a proposal of marriage or hand-fasting.

9 drops juniper berry oil
1 teaspoon hawthorn berry tincture
1 pinch sugar
1/2 ounce grape seed oil
1/2 ounce olive oil

Dissolve just a pinch of sugar into a tincture of hawthorn berry, then add a teaspoon of the tincture to the other ingredients.

Indra Oil

Used to anoint the ankles of soldiers entering battle. This is a good oil to use in combination with rites to combat all types of opposition to your intent.

12 drops cedar wood
9 drops petitgrain
1/2 ounce olive oil

Jupiter Oil

Anoint a green candle and then burn the candle during rites in which you wish nature to provide a needed resource.

9 drops galbanum oil
6 drops cypress oil
6 drops cedar wood oil
1/2 ounce almond oil

Mars Oil (Protection and Fertility)

Anoint a red candle and burn for protection or a green candle and burn for fertility.

9 drops opoponax (sweet myrrh) oil
6 drops benzoin oil
3 drops black pepper oil
1/2 ounce olive oil

Mars Oil (War and Both Offensive and Defensive Force)

Use as you would Ares oil.

9 drops dragon's blood perfume oil
6 drops black pepper oil
6 drops benzoin oil
1/2 ounce olive oil

Mercury Oil

Place a drop or two on the tires of your car or truck to ward off accidents. Also diffused to assist in communication.

11 drops lavender oil
9 drops lemongrass oil
1/2 ounce almond or olive oil

Minos Oil

Diffuse to assist in making decisions that concern people who look up to you.

21 drops galbanum oil
1/4 ounce olive oil

Odin Oil (non-death products)

I often work a few drops of this oil into my pottery and sculpture works, as it promotes artistic expression and the cunning that is often needed to work with challenging mediums.

9 drops benzoin oil
6 drops cedar wood oil
1/2 ounce almond oil or olive oil

Use almond oil as the base when it is wisdom and the father aspect that you wish to draw. Use olive oil if it is the warrior aspect. Odin is also heavily associated with both ambergris oil and musk oil (both death products).

Osiris Oil

Anoint objects and representations of ideas you wish to bring back to life. This is an excellent oil to anoint gardening tools.

12 drops benzoin oil
18 drops acacia tincture
1/4 ounce olive oil

Pan Oil

Anoint your inner thighs when looking for a sex partner, but not necessarily a love interest.

9 drops pine oil
6 drops myrrh oil
3 drops patchouli oil
1/2 ounce olive oil

Pluto Oil

Anoint your temples to assist in decisions of earthly wealth.

9 drops frankincense oil
6 drops peppermint oil
6 drops cypress oil
1/2 ounce olive oil

Poseidon Oil

Combine with Poseidon incense and make an offering during sea travel to assure safe passage.

9 drops cedar wood oil
6 drops myrrh oil
1/2 ounce olive oil

Priapus Oil

Anoint the inner thighs to promote sexual fertility.

9 drops pine oil
6 drops myrrh oil
1/2 ounce olive oil

Set Oil

Add to Set incense or sprinkle by itself. This oil is most often used to protect a border or property line. It can be used on doorways and other entry points to protect that which is within.

11 drops patchouli oil
9 drops myrrh oil
1/2 ounce base oil

Shiva Oil

Anoint tools of both destruction and creation, like the tools used to clear a field for gardening. Also used to stimulate the male sex drive by diffusing.

9 drops dragon's blood perfume oil
6 drops geranium oil
1/2 ounce base oil

Shu Oil

Used to anoint the wand and censor.

12 drops jasmine absolute
18 drops damiana tincture
6 drops gum arabic tincture
1/2 ounce base oil

Silvanus Oil

Anoint the hands prior to clearing an area of nature for ritual or doing the same for the building of a home or other sacred space.

9 drops juniper berry oil
6 drops pine oil
1/2 ounce olive oil

Surya Oil

Anoint the temples when attempting to increase your ability to compromise a position, especially with your wife or lover.

9 drops frankincense oil
6 drops cinnamon oil
1/2 ounce sunflower oil

Thoth Oil

Anoint the paper that you write on to combat writer's block. Anoint your hands and fingers lightly if you use a keyboard. Also, anoint a yellow candle and burn when it is his wisdom that you seek to draw upon.

12 drops benzoin
18 drops vervain tincture
6 drops gum arabic tincture
1/2 ounce base oil

Zeus Oil

Anoint a brown candle and burn with the intent of acquiring the stability needed to be a good father. Also diffuse when making fatherly decisions, especially about the punishment of children.

9 drops galbanum oil
6 drops jasmine absolute
1/2 ounce base oil

Oils of the planets

These oils are used in conjunction with specific intent when attempting to draw on their archetypal patterns as explained in Chapter 9. They are also used to charge talismans and other objects used to achieve the intent of their association.

Sol (Sun) Oil

9 drops bergamot oil
6 drops chamomile oil
6 drops cinnamon oil
1/2 ounce sunflower oil

Best if made on a Sunday, during the hour that falls in between the time of dawn and dusk, or during the planetary hour.

Luna (Moon) Oil

9 drops camphor oil
3 drops eucalyptus oil
3 drops lemon oil
3 drops myrrh oil
3 drops sandalwood oil
1/2 ounce grape seed oil

Best if made on a Monday night, during the planetary hour or when the moon is full.

Mars Oil

6 drops dragon's blood perfume oil
6 drops allspice berry oil
6 drops basil oil
3 drops coriander seed oil
1/2 ounce base oil

Best if made on a Tuesday during the planetary hour. This oil is greatly improved if you gently warm the base oil while dissolving dragon's blood resin into the oil and then using that oil as the base.

Mercury Oil

9 drops lemongrass oil
6 drops bergamot oil
3 drops lavender oil
3 drops clove oil
1/2 ounce almond oil

Best if made on a Wednesday, during one of the daylight planetary hours.

Jupiter Oil

9 drops juniper berry oil
6 drops clove oil
6 drops nutmeg oil
3 drops pine oil
3 drops sage oil
1/2 ounce olive oil

Best if made on a Thursday, during one of the daylight planetary hours.

Venus Oil

9 drops bergamot oil
9 drops rose oil
3 drops ylang-ylang oil
1/2 ounce base oil

Best if made on a Friday, during one of the nighttime planetary hours.

Saturn Oil

9 drops patchouli oil
6 drops myrrh oil
6 drops cypress oil
1/2 ounce base oil

Best if made on a Saturday, during one of the nighttime planetary hours.

Oils of the astrological signs

Astrological oils are most often used to attune representative items to a person's astrological sign. This better helps you to associate the representation of a person with the person. However, in every case where an astrological oil is used to attune a representative item to a person, you will have better luck if you can identify an oil or perfume that they wear frequently, as this will better make the connection in your mind. These oils are also useful in making deliberate change to your internal self. After determining the traits that you would like to include in your life, refer to an astrological guide to find out which signs are associated with those attributes. Wear that sign's oil as a personal perfume while you consider the attributes and how you can incorporate them into your life.

These oils are also very useful in the creation of personal power candles. Make the candle using a combination of normal candle-making instructions, the directions listed in the beginning of this chapter, and common sense. Burn personal power candles whenever you need an extra lift in your day-to-day life. This can be done within the confines of a Wiccan ritual or (if management permits) even on your desk at work.

Where a masculine or feminine version of the oil is listed, it is best to use the gender that aligns with the person's sex. Where a distinction has not been made, the practice should be overlooked.

Aquarius Oil (masculine)

9 drops peppermint oil
6 drops pine oil
1/2 ounce masculine base oil

Aquarius Oil (feminine)

9 drops cypress oil
9 drops patchouli oil
1/2 ounce famine base oil

Aries Oil

9 drops allspice berry oil
6 drops cinnamon oil
6 drops clove oil
1/2 ounce base oil

Cancer Oil (masculine)

9 drops palmarosa oil
6 drops chamomile absolute
1/2 ounce masculine base oil

Cancer Oil (feminine)

9 drops sandalwood oil
3 drops lemon oil
3 drops myrrh oil
3 drops jasmine absolute
1/2 ounce coconut oil*

You will probably have to gently warm the coconut oil for this blend to mix properly.

Capricorn Oil

9 drops patchouli oil
6 drops cypress oil
6 drops myrrh oil
1/2 ounce famine base oil

Gemini Oil

9 drops benzoin oil
6 drops lemongrass oil
6 drops peppermint oil
3 drops lavender oil
1/2 ounce almond oil

Leo Oil (masculine)

6 drops frankincense oil
6 drops bay oil
6 drops juniper berry oil
3 drops cinnamon oil
1/2 ounce sunflower oil

Leo Oil (feminine)

15 drops sandalwood oil
6 drops rosemary oil
1/2 ounce sunflower oil

Libra Oil (masculine)

9 drops peppermint oil
6 drops fennel seed oil
3 drops chamomile oil
3 drops thyme oil
1/2 ounce apricot kernel oil

Libra Oil (feminine)

9 drops eucalyptus oil
6 drops geranium oil
3 drops rose oil or spearmint oil
1/2 ounce apricot kernel oil

Pisces Oil

9 drops cardamom seed oil
6 drops clove oil
3 drops myrrh oil
3 drops sandalwood oil
1/2 ounce base oil

Sagittarius Oil

6 drops sage oil
6 drops orange oil
6 drops sweet grass oil
3 drops clove oil
1/4 base oil

Scorpio Oil

9 drops clove oil
6 drops black pepper oil
6 drops ginger oil
1/2 ounce olive oil

Taurus Oil

6 drops cardamom seed oil
3 drops patchouli oil
3 drops rose oil
3 drops thyme oil
1/2 ounce apricot kennel oil

Virgo Oil

6 drops patchouli oil
3 drops cypress oil
3 drops fennel seed oil
3 drops lavender oil
1/2 ounce olive oil

Elemental oils

These oils are most often used to anoint the Quarter candles and to anoint their corresponding tools. They are also used in conjunction with drawing on specific elemental energy. Use them to anoint the Quarter candles, or incorporate them into the actual making of your candles.

Earth Oil

12 drops patchouli oil
9 drops bergamot oil
1/2 ounce any base oil

Air Oil

9 drops benzoin oil
9 drops lavender oil
3 drops pine oils pine oil
1/2 ounce almond or palm oil

Fire Oil

6 drops allspice berry oil
3 drop bay oil
3 drops ginger oil
1/2 ounce any base oil

Water Oil

6 drops camphor oil
3 drops lemon oil
3 drops eucalyptus oil
3 drops cardamom seed oil
1/2 ounce any base oil

Oils of the chakras and primary colors

If you study the chakras in any depth, you will find that their color correspondence is not always the same from one book to the next. Recognizing the diversity on which we can draw our lore, I have made an effort to associate the chakras directly to the primary colors. There are actually many other chakras and energy points, just as there are many other colors. These oils are used to activate the energy centers of the body, and to strengthen the aura, as discussed in Chapter 4. They can also be placed in a diffuser and used to establish an atmosphere corresponding to the attributes listed in Chapter 9. If you use these oils in the making of candles, color those candles appropriately.

Red/Root Chakra

6 drops frankincense oil
6 drops myrrh oil
3 drops patchouli oil
1/2 cup almond oil

Orange/Sacral Chakra

9 drops sandalwood oil
6 drops rose or rose geranium oil
3 drops jasmine absolute
1/2 ounce almond oil

Yellow/Solar Plexus Chakra

6 drops lemon eucalyptus oil and 3 drops lemon oil
   (or 9 drops lemon oil)
6 drops basil oil
3 drops sage oil
1/2 ounce almond oil

Green/Heart Chakra

6 drops bergamot oil
6 drops geranium oil
3 drops neroli oil
3 drops rose oil
1/2 ounce almond oil

Blue/Throat Chakra

12 drops neroli oil
6 drops chamomile absolute
1/2 ounce almond oil

Indigo/Third Eye Chakra

12 drops lavender oil
6 drops rosemary oil
1/2 ounce almond oil

Violet/Crown Chakra

9 drops frankincense oil
6 drops lavender oil
6 drops sandalwood oil
1/2 ounce almond oil

Intent oils

The most common use of these oils is the anointing of candles and objects in correspondence with their specific intent.

Astral Travel Oil

Place a drop or two on each temple when attempting to enter the astral world.

13 drops benzoin oil
5 drops cinnamon oil
2 drops lavender oil
1/2 ounce jojoba

Banishing Oil

Use to cleanse objects of negative energy. Paranoid types might keep a bottle of this on the altar for emergencies. Should you encounter forces you wish to drive out, tossing a few drops into a censor of charcoal will generate a response more quickly than incense.

9 drops clove oil
6 drops juniper berry oil
6 drops pine oil
1/2 ounce base oil

Business Success

Place a piece of malachite in a purple sachet in each corner and add a drop or two of this oil to the sachet once a week.

9 drops cinnamon oil
6 drops basil oil
3 drops clove oil
3 drops patchouli oil
1/2 ounce olive oil

Celibacy Oil for Men

Fill a white sachet with celibacy incense and a few drops of this oil and carry it with you. When you feel tempted, inhale its scent. I have noted that this recipe simply does not work in candles. The scent remains strong, but so do natural desires. Perhaps the association between sex and candlelight is entirely too strong for it to overcome.

6 drops camphor oil
3 drops lavender oil
1/2 ounce base coconut or other base oil
Coconut oil is the perfect base for this mixture, but others will do.

Courage Oil

15 drops frankincense oil
6 drops black pepper oil
1/2 ounce base oil

Divination Oil (expensive)

Place one drop on each temple when meditating. This is not a good recipe to use in candles.

9 drops jasmine oil
9 drops rose oil
3 drops orange oil
1/2 ounce base oil

Divination (affordable)

Place one drop on each temple when meditating. This is excellent oil to use in candles that will be used for divination.

6 drops bergamot oil
6 drops cypress oil
3 drops clove oil
1/2 ounce base oil

Dreams Oil (to bring)

Place three drops on your pillow or the head of your bed and one on each temple.

9 drops lavender oil
6 drops sage oil
1/2 ounce base oil

Energy Oil (physical)

Carry in pocket on a cloth swab for the time that you need a little extra energy in your stride. Astrologically based oils are better for psychic energy.

6 drops camphor oil
6 drops cinnamon oil
6 drops patchouli or orange oil
1/2 ounce sunflower oil

Friendship Oil

Wear as a perfume to ease tension between friends and potential friends. Anoint a yellow ribbon and tie it in a bow at the entrance to your door. Invite friends to touch it as they enter. This blend also seems to combat shyness.

6 drops benzoin oil
6 drops orange oil
3 drops petitgrain oil
1/2 ounce of base oil

Healing Oil

Diffuse during healing mediations and rituals.

9 drops eucalyptus oil
6 drops allspice berry oil
6 drops juniper berry oil
1/2 cup olive oil

Joy/Anti-Depression

Rub a few drops into the temples. Also works well as a relaxing massage oil. Be aware that if it promotes headaches, you are probably allergic to ylang-ylang oil.

9 drops sage oil
6 drops basil oil
3 drops ylang-ylang oil
1/2 ounce almond oil (2 ounces if used as a massage oil)

Love (for a woman to feel)

Diffuse into the air or use as a love-drawing massage oil. Wear as a personal perfume to promote the feeling of love in women who smell it.

6 drops lemon oil
6 drops cardamom seed oil
3 drops spearmint oil
1/2 ounce almond oil (2 ounces if used as a massage oil)

Love Oil (premium and general)

This is also a mood-setting oil. Diffuse it into the air to promote romantic love in both men and women. Dilute it as instructed, and this makes incredible massage oil for romantic evenings. Remember that there is a clear difference between love and lust.

9 drops rose oil
3 drops jasmine oil
1/2 ounce almond oil (2 ounces if used as a massage oil)

Love (for a man to feel)

Diffuse to lighten a heavy heart.
9 drops dragon's blood perfume oil
6 drops rose oil (rose geranium is acceptable)
6 drops lavender oil
1/4 ounce

Luck Oil (general)

When used in candles or diffused into the air, the scent of this blend instills a feeling of luck when its subtle scent is noticed by either the conscious or subconscious mind.

9 drops bergamot oil
6 drops allspice berry oil
6 drops orange oil
1/2 ounce base oil

Lust Oil (to inspire lust in a woman for a man)

Wear on the body as you would a perfume. When used as a massage oil, this is very inspiring.

9 drops patchouli oil
6 drops sandalwood oil
3 drops rose oil
1/2 ounce sunflower oil (2 ounces of almond oil if used for massage)

Lust Oil (to inspire lust in a man for a woman)

Wear on the body as you would a personal perfume.

9 drops neroli oil
6 drops ginger oil
1/2 ounce apricot seed oil

Meditation Oil

Massage a drop into each temple. This is excellent but expensive oil to use when making meditation candles.

9 drops frankincense oil
6 drops sandalwood oil
3 drops myrrh oil
1/2 ounce almond oil

Memory Oil

The difference between a fairytale and a war story is that a fairytale starts off "once upon a time" and a war story starts off "and this ain't no bull." This oil will help you remember both when old friends drop by. It also is a great study oil. Diffuse it while you study and add a few drops to a cloth. When taking that hard test, hold the cloth to your face and inhale deeply. Like popcorn and the movie theater, any scent has the ability to stir memories of the last time you smelled it, but this one works very well. Any chant that will be used with this oil should be one directly associated with what memories you are trying to stir. In the case of the war stories, military cadence will do fine.

9 drops rosemary oil
9 drops peppermint oil
3 drops juniper oil
1/2 ounce base oil

Prosperity Oil

This oil should be used in conjunction with all activities in which you hope to prosper. Wear it on the wrists as you conduct yourself in a manner that is deserving of a raise at work. If Lotto is your game, anoint your lottery ticket but remember that even if it cuts your odds in half, you are still facing only a shot in millions. Better to use it in conjunction with less risk-based endeavors.

9 drops patchouli oil
6 drops cinnamon oil
3 drops orange oil
3 drops clove oil
1/2 almond oil base

Protection Oil (general)

Used to anoint self for strength against psychic attacks and to anoint objects to charge them as talismans of protection. I received this recipe from a friend who routinely anointed his flack jacket with this mixture when he was a Marine. As the result of a car bomb, his left arm was torn all but loose from his body. Even with almost full use of the limb after it was re-attached, the Marines would not let him re-enlist, so he joined the Army, where we met. He still swore by the oil because he survived. After telling this story to a friend who is a police officer, she let me place a few drops on the soft armor of her bulletproof vest. A month later, she was shot with a rifle cartridge. Even though she was not wearing the hard plate inserts that are designed to stop rifle rounds, the bullet did not penetrate her chest. Yes, she did have one heck of a bruise and, as I recall, one of her ribs was broken, but she survived. Anointing your wrists will not stop a bullet, but it might help you to remember your bulletproof vest or recognize a threat quick enough to get out of its killing zone.

6 drops cypress oil
6 drops patchouli
6 drops rose oil
1/2 ounce almond oil

Purification Oil #1 (generally for objects)

I prefer to make all of my own magickal tools, but every now and then I find something in an antique mall or flea market that feels absolutely right. Even so, I use this or a like blend to get rid of the psychic sludge that sometimes rides in on used goods. Rub a few drops on any surface that will not be damaged by oil. If the object is water safe, mix this with sea salt and a little bit of laundry detergent for a cleansing bath.

The detergent will act as an emulsifier and allow the water and oil to mix.

6 drops bay oil
6 drops benzoin oil
3 drops cinnamon oil
3 drops clove oil
1/2 ounce olive oil

Purification Oil #2 (generally for self and personal environments)

The home is sacred space. As such, you should avoid asking anyone into it that you do not feel comfortable with. Unfortunately, we do not always have the luxury of being the only one who makes such decisions. In my case, this is the case with my roommate's girlfriend's mother. When it comes to psychic sludge, the woman is a leaking 55-gallon drum. Not only does this oil saturate my diffuser when she leaves; I try to remember to place it there in anticipation of her arrival.

9 drops frankincense oil
3 drops cinnamon oil
3 drops bay oil
1/2 ounce olive oil

Sexual Energy (in men)

Of all places to put an oil with such a name, this seems to work best on your socks. To be effective for nighttime romps, place it there in the morning and wear it during the day. Then take a shower, change your clothes (especially your socks), and use an oil more befitting your partner. The psychic impression of this oil will last for many hours.

6 drops allspice berry oil
6 drops dragon's blood perfume oil
6 rosemary oil

Strength (physical)

This works best as a massage oil when used in conjunction with deep muscle massage, but it is also used in diffusers. If you are an employer, a sneaky use of this oil is to diffuse it into the workplace when your employees will have a particularly physically active day. This is no more manipulative than providing employees with free coffee, even the scent of which has been shown to increase performance.

9 drops lemongrass oil
6 drops sandalwood oil
6 drops nutmeg oil
1/2 ounce almond oil (2 ounces if massage oil)

Success Oil (general)

The scent of this oil encourages people towards the attributes that bring success. This oil is not worn on the body. Instead, try diffusing it at the workplace or placing a few drops on the cuff of your pant legs. Be warned that excessive use will eat at the fabric.

9 drops ginger oil
6 drops cinnamon oil
1/2 ounce sunflower kernel oil

Unstress Oil

Diffuse this into the air when you want to relax. Note that this oil does not contain fillers or carrier oils. Be especially careful not to get this on your skin.

2 parts lavender oil
1 part benzoin oil
1 part cumin seen oils

Wisdom Oil

This scent tends to promote contemplation and consideration before action. It is diffused, used in candles, and worn on the temples.

6 drops frankincense oil
6 drops sandalwood oil
3 drops sage oil
1/2 ounce almond oil

Wishing Oil

Anoint a ribbon selected with an appropriate color (see Chapter 9 under chakras), write your wish on a piece of parchment paper, as many times as will fit, on both sides. Roll up the parchment paper and tie it with the ribbon. Burn this outdoors and see your wishes rise up with the smoke and ash. As you do so, recite your wish over and over. Do this each day until you receive your wish.

9 drops sage oil
9 drops sandalwood oil
1/2 ounce base oil

Miscellaneous Magickal Lore

Gold and garbage

Y ou cannot possibly follow the scientific method to determine each and every spell that is associated with each of your intents. On the other hand, you should not believe everything you read. Instead, you must find a comfortable area in between determining your own lore and trusting lore that has been listed elsewhere. This chapter lists many of the associations that have worked for me.

When I was first shown a list of associations, it was handwritten with no attempt at a bibliography. If I wanted the information, I had to copy it by hand, word by word. When I asked why I couldn't have it photocopied, I was told that it is tradition that the student copies the work by hand. I did, even though I thought the whole process was silly. Later, I found that this "tradition," like many other pointless traditions, can be tracked to Gardnerian and his now infamous writings. It was reportedly a way of compartmentalizing individuals so that if one were caught during the burning times, their writings would not give up the others in their covens/cells. If others wanted to copy your information, you were not to write it out yourself, because if they were caught with that material, you might be identified by your handwriting.

When I asked why the associations were made, I was told only that they were tradition. I have found tradition to be a funny thing. It is very much like gold or garbage. Either way, tradition tends to hold its starting value over time, but when it is garbage, it starts to stink quickly.

Since that time, I have used the results of experimentation to change, add to, and take away from what I was originally shown. That is the way it should be. The only one who knows what will work for you is you.

In researching this book, I compared many different sources of like material and found one very interesting correlation. Most literature on the subject agrees almost completely with *777* by Aleister Crowley. This is so much so that in *A Witches' God,* authors Janet and Stewart Farrar included direct notation of their source material at each point it was referenced. However, I am not so sure Aleister Crowley (1875-1947) was completely forthcoming with his sources because *777* does not contain a bibliography. Further research reveals that S.L. MacGregor Mathers (1854 - 1918) presented most of these associations to the Golden Dawn long before Crowley's *777*.

Some of my favorite God forms and associations

It would not be practical to list every god form to grace the minds of men. What I have listed are the ones that have graced this man's mind. These are my friends, inspirations, and warnings. I encourage you to discover and experiment with god forms from all cultures. Ultimately, you will pick your own friends and archetypes.

An asterisk (*) notes an item whose procurement involves the killing of an animal. Although these oils have their use in lore, I do not feel they should be used in a religion that celebrates life. Yes, for life there must be death. But death for perfume seems to cross the line of necessity. You decide what is right for you.

Adonis [Greek]

Vegetation, cycles and patterns, resurrection, restoration, balance.

Adonis was hidden in the underworld by Persephone. When he was accidentally killed, Aphrodite asked Zeus to bring him back for her alone. Zeus decided Adonis would spend the Winter half of the year with Persephone in Hades, but that he would spend the Summer half of the year with Aphrodite.

Associated Plant(s): acacia, bay, lily, myrrh, rose.

Associated Precious Mineral(s): topaz, yellow diamond, peridot.

Associated Concentrations and Extract(s): acacia (tincture), bay (oil), myrrh (oil), and rose (oil).

Associated Base Oil(s): jojoba and olive oil.

Aeacus [Greek]

Integrity, good judgment, honesty, negotiations, identification of truth.

When Hera went on one of her tantrums, Aeacus negotiated help from Zeus. When Aeacus died, Zeus made him one of three judges of the underworld.

Associated Plant(s): aloe, frankincense, allspice, cinnamon.

Associated Concentrations and Extract(s): allspice berry (oil), cinnamon (oil), and frankincense (oil).

Agni [Hindu]

Fire energy, the embodiment of plants, fertility, male vitality.

Agni is a Hindu Fire god. His lightning bolt brought rain to make the land fertile. One can easily see the symbolism between the phallus (lightning) and semen (rain). With this symbolism, we can see how Agni was a fertility god.

Associated Plants(s): dragon's blood resin, hibiscus, nettle, poppy.

Associated Mineral(s): opal.

Associated Concentrations and Extract(s): dragon's blood (perfume oil), hibiscus (tincture), nettle (tincture), and poppy (tincture).

Apollo [Greek / Roman]

Prophesy, sun, warmth, light, truth, medicine, poetry, fine arts.

At one point, Apollo was seen as controlling each of the muses. He is an accomplished musician, an Olympic athlete, and a very accurate archer. He is depicted in ancient art more frequently than any other single god, possibly because he was described as beautiful.

Associated Plant(s): acacia, bay, cypress, fenugreek, lily of the valley, lotus, mistletoe, olive, palm and its fruit the date, sunflower, thistle.

Associated Mineral(s): alexandrite, tourmaline, sapphire.

Associated Concentrations and Extract(s): acacia (tincture), bay (oil), cypress (oil), and wormwood (tincture).

Associated Base Oil(s): olive and sunflower oil.

Ares [Greek]

Victory, violence, aggressive, personification of war.

Ares is first and foremost a god of war. He is often overlooked in Wiccan traditions for this reason. Before you dismiss this important god form, consider what it took to free the Jews from Hitler's concentration camps and end further suffering. It took a war. Would this book be published without the Bill of Rights to assure freedom of the press? Would Americans have such an assurance without the Revolutionary War?

Associated Plant(s): benzoin, dragon's blood, nettle, rue, wormwood.

Associated Mineral(s): iron, sulfur.

Associated Concentrations and Extract(s): benzoin (tincture), dragon's blood (perfume oil), wormwood (tincture).

Asclepius [Greek]

Healing, medicine, health.

Asclepius was a physician of such quality that the underworld became entirely too unpopulated. To solve the problem, Zeus killed him with a lightning bolt. His temples and hospitals were usually one in the same. I would say the moral of this story is that Zeus is not a very good god form to call on for healings.

Associated Plant(s): bay, juniper, lily of the valley, mustard.

Associated Mineral(s): agate (especially red agate).

Associated Concentrations and Extract(s): bay (oil), juniper berry (oil), mustard seed (tincture).

Associated Base Oil(s): olive and/or grapeseed oil.

Bacchus [Roman]

Wine, vegetation, indulgence, cheer, destruction, insanity.

Originally known as Dionysus, the name Bacchus surfaced around 400 B.C.E. It is a reference to the cheering that was offered up to Dionysus during worship at the orgia. Both are gods of wine and indulgence. He is kind to those who are of like minds, but brings madness and destruction to those who are not. I look at it like this: His name is Dionysus, but his friends call him Bacchus.

Associated Plant(s): grape, ivy, thistle, patchouli.

Associated Mineral(s): black diamond.

Associated Extracts and Concentration(s): civit (oil)*, musk (oil)*, patchouli (oil), thistle (tincture).

Associate Base Oil(s): grapeseed oil.

Brahma [Hindu]

Connectivity with your female half.

Brahma is typically listed as having the attribute of balance. I wholly disagree. He separated himself into both male (Purusha/Skambha) and female (Skambha). From the sexual union of his two halves, came the birth of Saravati, who became his wife.

Associated Plant(s): ash, cedar, cypress, fig, hyssop, ivy, oak, olive, poplar.

Associated Mineral(s): amethyst, sapphire, lapis lazuli.

Associated Extracts and Concentration(s): cedar wood (oil), cypress (oil), hyssop (tincture).

Associated Base Oil(s): olive oil.

Chandra [Hindu]

Vegetation, fertility, conception.

Chandra is the original Hindu moon god. He was later merged with Soma. He is a god of vegetation fertility, especially crops and medicinal plants. The morning dew comes from Chandra (the moon) to help plants grow. He was one of the Vasus (a tribe of gods who held Indhra as its chief). Pray to him when you want to have a child.

Associated Plant(s): almond, mugwort.

Associated Mineral(s): moonstone, all crystals, especially quartz.

Associated Extracts and Concentration(s): camphor (oil).

Associated base oil(s): Almond oil.

Cupid [Roman]

Love, healthy relationship with your mother.

Cupid is not only a god of love, he has a wonderful relationship with his mother, Venus. We are not really sure who his father is. Venus will only say that it is either Mars (god of war) or Mercury (god of communication). This is very interesting when we consider the nature of love, communication, or war. Maybe it was a little of both.

Associated Plant(s): cypress, juniper berry, rose.

Associated Mineral(s): opal.

Associated Extracts and Concentration(s): cypress (oil), juniper berry (oil), rose (oil).

Associated Base Oil(s): olive oil.

Dagda, The [Irish]

Father figure, sexual potency, fertility, abundance, fierce in combat.

I love this god. The Dagda is a father figure, but not in the sense that you are a child. More in the sense that he is your father/buddy, the guy who buys your first beer. He is a down-to-earth sort of god, willing to laugh at himself and let others do the same. He is often shown with a pot belly and not always in the best of clothes, just like many of us. But when he is called to protect his own, he is fierce. It takes nine mortal men to lift his battle club. He is the embodiment of the scoundrel. After visiting the camp of an enemy under a flag of truce, he slept with the enemy's women and convinced one of them to use her magick against her own people.

Associated Plant(s): oak.

Associated Extracts and Concentration(s): heather (tincture), hops (tincture).

Dianus [Roman]

Fertility, deep forests.

Dianus is the horned god that people seem to have forgotten. Dianus was created when Diana separated herself into darkness (female) and light (male). Diana tried everything she could to attract his sexual desires, but he refused and refused until she tricked him into giving of his seed. From that treachery came Aradia. It is interesting to note that although Dianus predates Lucifer, the story is most often told with Lucifer as Diana's brother/lover. Maybe the shock value gets more attention.

Associated Plant(s): oak.

Dionysus [Greek]

Wine, vegetation, indulgence, cheer, destruction, insanity, rebirth, self-sacrifice.

His friends call him Bacchus. Although you might think you know him, you couldn't be further from the truth. Yes, he does drink a bit and he is a bastard by the very definition of the word, but he has gone out of his way to help others time and time again. He met his wife when Theseus abandoned her. He went all the way to Hades to rescue his own mother.

Associated Plant(s): fennel, fig, grape, ivy, juniper, patchouli, pine.

Associated Extracts and Concentration(s): juniper berry (oil), patchouli (oil), pine (oil).

Associated Base Oil(s): grapeseed oil.

Eros [Greek]

Love, harmony, creativity, mischief, wanderlust, relationships of all kinds.

Eros is the god of love. Like his Roman equivalent (Cupid), his nature is not always as clear as could be. Just like love, he can be harmonious and creative. But he can also be tremendously mischievous. Don't ever expect him to do what you think. He is very fond of poetic justice. His wanderlust might explain why an asteroid was named after him in 1898.

Associated Plant(s): bay, rose, yarrow.

Associated Extracts and Concentration(s): bay (oil), rose (oil), yarrow (tincture).

Associated Base Oil(s): olive oil.

Faunus [Roman]

All things in nature, common interests, divination, prophetic dreams, sexual union, setting down rules.

He and his wife Fauna make a cute couple. She is a goddess of the Earth and fields. He is a nature god. Could there be a better match? He is great with solving relationship issues and bringing men and women together. When he is working in that capacity, he is called Lupercus. His annual festival, Lupercalia (February 15), is probably the origins of Saint Valentine's day.

Associated Plant(s): bay, pine.

Associated Extracts and Concentration(s): bay (oil), pine (oil).

Ganesa [Hindu]

Good fortune, wisdom, literature, strategy, intelligence, intuition, joy, popularity.

For many years, we kept a huge aquarium with rescued rats in my store. We were routinely asked if we sacrificed the rats to Satan. "Why no" I would answer. "We sacrifice peanuts to the rats in honor of Ganesa." I received the strangest looks. He is one of the smartest gods I know. Go to him when you are having difficulty in logic. But be careful about involving him in anything that has to do with love.

The woman you are thinking about might not be as understanding as Ganesa's two wives.

Associated Plant(s): damiana, jasmine, sesame, peanuts.

Associated Mineral(s): lead.

Associated Extracts and Concentration(s): damiana (tincture), jasmine (absolute).

Associated Base Oil(s): sesame oil, peanut oil.

Hades [Greek]

(See also Pluto) Wealth of the Earth, learned fidelity, stability.

Hades is another god that is often misunderstood. Yes, he did kidnap Persephone, but he did it out of love. He later proved to be one of the most faithful of the Olympian gods, having cheated only twice. Compare that to Persephone's response, and you can figure out who is the heavy is in this relationship. When Persephone caught Hades cheating the first time, she beat his nymph lover into the ground and then turned her into a mint plant. She probably would have done worse to the second lover, but she was Poseidon's daughter and you know how he can be about his daughters. Remember, he is the keeper of the underworld from where most riches come.

Hades is an important god form for men in relationships. Monogomy is not always the norm. As long as everyone is happy with whatever sexual behavior goes on within a relationship, then problems are few. But when someone is dishonest about their intent or conduct, problems are grand and many. What is standard social conduct on Mount Olympus is not always standard social conduct in Indiana.

Associated Plant(s): frankincense, hibiscus, nettle, oak, poppy.

Associated Mineral(s): ruby, fire opal, iron, sulphur.

Associated Extracts and Concentration(s): frankincense (oil), poppy (tincture), hibiscus (tincture), nettle (tincture).

Associated Base Oil(s): olive oil.

Hanuman [Hindu]

Ability to learn, cunning, all other skills of the mind.

If you need help in your studies, Hanuman is an excellent choice of tutors. His cunning and intelligence was key in the rescue of Sita.

Associated Plant(s): benzoin, gum mastic, mace, sandalwood, vervain.

Associated Mineral(s): fire opal (regular opal will due), agate.

Associated Extracts and Concentration(s): benzoin (tincture or oil), gum mastic (tincture), nutmeg (oil), sandalwood (oil), mace (tincture).

Helios [Greek]

Blessings to polyamourous relationships, illumination of understanding, sexual stamina, fertility, light, warmth.

Helios and his many wives seem to get along fine. Polyamourus relationships don't always go so well, but with his help, you can learn to place your heart before your jealousy.

Associated Plant(s): frankincense, cinnamon, sunflower.

Associated Mineral(s): chrysoleth.

Associated Extracts and Concentration(s): frankincense (oil), cinnamon (oil).

Associated Base Oil(s): sunflower oil.

Hermes [Greek]

Intellect, communication, commerce, travel, sexual prowess.

He's great with the lady folk because he is smart and funny. His occasional practical jokes can be a tad bit on the annoying side, but his company is well worth the risk. Hermes is great for resolving disputes by opening the paths to communication. He is a businessman's dream partner, although he doesn't always offer the customer a fair deal. This might be why he is also reputed to give luck to thieves.

Associated Plant(s): benzoin, gum mastic, mace, sandalwood, vervain.

Associated Mineral(s): opal, agate, mercury.

Associated Extracts and Concentration(s): benzoin (tincture), mastic (oil), sandalwood (oil).

Associated Base Oil(s): olive oil.

Herne [Celtic]

Male sexual potency, animals, fertility, life, wealth, transition to death.

Also called Cernunnos, he is the horned god. He is the embodiment of the principal male deity form in most pagan and neopagan traditions. Because we no longer rely on the hunt for our food, he is greatly misunderstood. His association is not just god of the literal hunting of animals. He is the god of providing for your tribe, family, and household. He is the god of finding a new job (job hunting), of sacrificing long hours of overtime so the kids can have extra special Yule gifts this year. If we continue to associate him with the literal hunting of food, Homer Simpson might as well be our god of the hunt and his altar could be a box of doughnuts.

It is interesting to note that there is a city in west central Germany by the same name, as well as many geographical locations that use the name Herne or derivatives of it.

Associated Plant(s): oak, patchouli, pine.

Associated Extracts and Concentration(s): *civit (oil), *musk (oil), patchouli (oil), pine (oil).

Horus [Egyptian]

Retribution, goodness, silence, secrets, honor, respect, anti-gossip.

Horus is a challenge to the common ideas of right and wrong. He is a god of goodness, but he avenged his father's death by killing his uncle. As Horus the Younger, he was also Harpocrates [Greek and Roman]. As Harpocrates, he stumbled onto the goddess Diana during one of her many adulterous adventures. Diana's son, Cupid, offered Harpocrates a single beautiful rose in exchange for his vow of silence. Harpocrates accepted and the rose became associated with silence. Harpocrates/Horus the Younger is typically viewed with a finger to his lips. During medieval times, a rose was sometimes hung over a banquet table to remind guests that what was spoken at the table should not be repeated elsewhere.

Associated Plant(s): dragon's blood, horehound, nettle, oak, rue, rose, sunflower, wormwood, yarrow.

Associated Mineral(s): ruby, iron, sulphur.

Associated Extracts and Concentration(s): black pepper (oil), dragon's blood (perfume oil), rose (oil), yarrow (oil).

Associated Base Oil(s): sunflower oil.

Hymen [Greek]

Celebrations of marriage and similar unions, pampering women.

Ah, the god form that is also a part of a female sex organ. Of course he is the god of marriage celebrations; his mother is Aphrodite (goddess of love) and his father is Dionysus (god of wine and indulgence). Who better to be your best man? Do not put him in charge of your bachelor party unless your bride to be is very open minded. This guy likes to party and he is a definite ladies' man. He is also a very good ally in the pampering, bathing, and general gentle care of women, but don't ever tell them that. If they find out he likes it, they will demand so much more.

Associated Plant(s): hawthorn, juniper.

Associated Extracts and Concentration(s): hawthorn berry (tincture), juniper berry (oil).

Associated Base Oil(s): grapeseed oil, olive oil.

Indra [Hindu]

Combat, defense, force, order, rain, thunder.

In Vedic times, Indra was the man. He ruled over all the Hindu gods and led the Devas. His strength and intelligence made him a very formidable warrior. He used his combat abilities to defend both man and god from forces that would do them harm. He is a fertility and creator god form because he brought water (fertility) to the earth and gave the world order (creator).

Associated Plant(s): aloe, olive, orange, saffron.

Associated Mineral(s): amethyst, sapphire, lapis lazuli.

Associated Extracts and Concentration(s): aloe vera (expressed), cedar wood (oil), orange (oil).

Associated Base Oil(s): olive oil.

Janus [Roman]

Change, opportunity.

Janus is the Roman god of doorways. If you need a change, he can show you the options. Put Janus down with the want ads, and you are sure to find a new job.

Associated Plant(s): oak.

Associated Mineral(s): phosphorus.

Associated Extracts and Concentration(s): *musk (oil), white oak bark (tincture).

Associated Base Oil(s): olive oil.

Jupiter [Roman]

Weather, agriculture, succession, protector of society and law, truth, justice, virtue.

After overthrowing the rule of his father, Saturn, Jupiter became the supreme Roman god form. So much was this the case that his role as agriculture god became overshadowed with the new responsibilities of state.

Associated Plant(s): almond, carnation, cypress, fig, gorse, hyssop, mullein, oak, olive, poplar, vervain.

Associated Extracts and Concentration(s): cedar wood (oil), cypress (oil), galbanum (oil), orange (oil).

Associated Base Oil(s): almond oil, olive oil.

Liber Pater [Roman]

Transition into manhood, fertility.

More than any other Roman fertility god form, Liber Pater is in charge of the passing into manhood. The actual crossing is typically marked on March 17, which is the day of his festival the Liberalias.

Associated Plant(s): almond, grape.

Lono [Polynesian]

Fertility, jealousy, regret.

The story of Lono and his love Kaikilani warns us of anger-management problems. When Lono doubted Kaikilani's fidelity, he became so controlled by anger that he killed her in a rage of violence. At the loss of his love by his own hands, he became insane with remorse and regret. This story has been repeated over and over, but men still do not seem to get it. Control your anger or your anger will control you.

Associated Plant(s): kava-kava, ti.

Mars [Roman]

War, protective father, crop fertility, desirous of similarities in mates.

Mars is the protective father, hence his other Roman name, Marspiter (Father Mars). Originally he was a crop fertility god form. His wife, Rhea Silvia, bore him twins, Romulus and Remus. After the twins founded Rome, Mars changed as he became more involved in the conquests of what became the Roman Empire. He was the protector of the field and later, a god of war, marching on the fields of other lands for the glory of Rome. As he changed, so did his love interests. His choice of lovers became women of similar interests in war, in particular, Bellona and Vacuna. Mars shows us that life is change.

Associated Plant(s): benzoin, coconut, dragon's blood, geranium, nettle, oak, olive, rue, vervain, wormwood.

Associated Mineral(s): ruby, iron, onyx, sulphur.

Associated Extracts and Concentration(s): black pepper (oil), benzoin (tincture and oil), dragon's blood (perfume oil), sweet myrrh (a.k.a. opoponax [oil]), wormwood (tincture).

Associated Base Oil(s): olive oil.

Mercury [Roman]

Communication, travel, retail sales, protection in flight.

Mercury, like Hermes, is a god form of merchants, but Mercury is less likely to put his thumb on the scale.

Associated Plant(s): almond, lemongrass, lavender, lotus, vervain, willow.

Associated Mineral(s): opal, agate, amber, mercury.

Associated Extracts and Concentration(s): lemongrass (oil), lavender (oil).

Associated Base Oil(s): almond oil, olive oil.

Minos [Greek]

Justice, judgment, expansion, revenge.

Minos is another god form that challenges conventional ideas of right and wrong. As the wise ruler of Crete, he expanded his domain to include many of the Aegean islands. Although he was widely considered a justice god, he was also vengeful. When his son, Androgeos, was killed by Athenians, he forced Athens to surrender youths and maidens for sacrifice to the minotaur.

Associated Plant(s): aloe.

Associated Mineral(s): emerald.

Associated Extracts and Concentration(s): aloe vera (expressed), galbanum (oil).

Associated Base Oil(s): olive oil.

Neptune [Roman]

Safe (fresh) water travel

Although Neptune is most often associated with the ocean, he was originally a god form of streams, ponds, and other sources of fresh water. It was only by association with the Greek god form, Poseidon, that he became associated with salt water.

Associated Plant(s): lotus, myrrh.

Associated Mineral(s): beryl, aquamarine.

Associated Concentrations and Extract(s): lotus (tincture), myrrh (oil), *ambergris (oil).

Associated Base Oil(s): olive oil. Also associated with *onycha in its many forms.

Odin [Norse]

Wisdom, poetry, magick, war, sacrifice.

Odin willingly surrendered in exchange for a drink at Mimir, the fountain of wisdom. Although typically thought limited to the form of god of war, he was also a god of wisdom, poetry and magick. He was known by many similar names, including Odhinn [Old Norse], Woden [Anglo-Saxon], Wodan/Woutan [Old High German], and my absolute favorite, Wotan [Teutonic].

Associated Plant(s): almond, cedar, benzoin, elm, mistletoe, olive.

Associated Mineral(s): amethyst, diamond, mercury, opal, phosphorus, sapphire, star ruby, turquoise.

Associated Extracts and Concentration(s): *ambergris (oil), cedar wood (oil), *musk (oil), benzoin (tincture or oil), mistletoe (tincture).

Associated Base Oil(s): almond oil, olive oil.

Osiris [Egyptian]

Fertility, transition, regeneration, recovery, afterlife, law, agriculture, music, singing, inventiveness.

Osiris represents the male productive and reproductive forces of nature. He was slain by his brother Set, who tore his body into 14 pieces, then scattered them across Egypt. Isis tracked down all but one of the pieces. His phallus had unfortunately been eaten by a crab. She fashioned a golden phallus with magick, then restored Osiris with the help of Anubis and Nephthys. The golden phallus must have worked. Upon his resurrection, Osiris gave his seed to Isis who then bore his son, Horus. Horus later killed Set out of revenge.

Associated Plant(s): acacia, benzoin, dittany of crete, ivy, orris, willow.

Associated Mineral(s): crystal, topaz, magnesium sulphate.

Associated Extracts and Concentration(s): acacia (tincture), benzoin (tincture or oil), dittany of crete (tincture), white willow bark (tincture).

Pan [Greek]

Provider, nature, woods, hunting, spelunking, natural adventures, hidden places, shepherds and flocks, panic.

Pan is the most common figure of the horned god. Like virtually all horned gods, Pan was a god of the hunt. This makes his modern reference the provider. The word *panic* comes from his name. Pan was said to cause unexplained panic in the hearts of those who ventured into his domain. Wouldn't it be nice to do the same to those who enter your domain?

Associated Plant(s): myrrh, oak, pine, thistle.

Associated Mineral(s): black diamond, carbon.

Associated Extracts and Concentration(s): myrrh (oil), pine (oil).

Associated Base Oil(s): olive oil.

Pluto [Roman]

Earth, stability, death, transition.

It is unfortunate that Pluto and his Greek counterpart, Hades, are so strongly associated with death when they have so much more to offer. In some pagan traditions, the three worlds are represented by sky, water, and Earth. In Wicca, this is can be seen in the three aspects of creation: father, mother, and children. Knowing that all land once came from the ocean and the ocean is often considered the womb of the Goddess, we can easily assign the role of Earth to the children of the Lord and Lady. What's this got to do with Pluto and Hades? Pluto and his two brothers, Neptune and Jupiter, conspired to overthrow their father's reign. Afterwards, they split all of creation into three domains. Neptune took the sea, Jupiter took the sky, and Pluto took the Earth. His very strong association with the Earth provides the link to stability.

Associated Plant(s): cypress, fig, frankincense, hibiscus, hyssop, nettle, oak, peppermint, poplar, poppy, saffron.

Associated Mineral(s): amethyst, lapis lazuli, fire opal, nitrates.

Associated Extracts and Concentration(s): cypress (oil), frankincense (oil), hibiscus (tincture), hyssop (tincture), nettle (tincture), white oak bark (tincture), peppermint (oil) poppy (tincture).

Associated Base Oil(s): olive oil.

Poseidon [Greek]

Safe (salt) water travel, earthquakes, revenge.

Poseidon helped build the walls around the city of Troy. After being cheated out of his wages for help with the wall, he took revenge on the city by first raising a sea monster against the land holdings of Troy, and then by backing the Greeks against them in the Trojan war.

Associated Plant(s): cedar, lotus, myrrh, olive.

Associated Mineral(s): amethyst, beryl, sapphire, aquamarine, sulfates.

Associated Extracts and Concentration(s): cedar wood (oil), lotus (tincture), myrrh (oil).

Associated Base Oil(s): olive oil. Also associated with *onycha in its many forms.

Priapus [Greek]

Agricultural fertility, work fertility.

Here's one to balance Mother Earth. In any place of agriculture, it was once common to come across a small statue of Priapus with a huge erect phallus. He also assists in fertility of thought, mind, and heart in the workplace.

Associated Plant(s): myrrh, pine, thistle.

Associated Mineral(s): black diamond.

Associated Extracts and Concentration(s): *musk (oil), *civit (oil), myrrh (oil), pine (oil), thistle (tincture).

Associated Base Oil(s): olive oil.

Ptah [Egyptian]

Creativity in craft, sculpting (especially in stone).

His name literally means "creator." In Egyptian lore, he was responsible for creating not only humans and the earth, but the spirits of the gods as well. He brought everything into existence by knowing its name.

Associated Plant(s): almond.

Associated Mineral(s): diamond.

Associated Extracts and Concentration(s): bitter almond (oil), *ambergris (oil).

Associated Base Oil(s): sweet almond oil.

Set [Egyptian]

Intelligence, destruction, tempering.

Wiccans claim they do not believe in Satan or the personification of evil. Most do not bat an eye if a woman draws Kali, but if a man draws Set, then there is hell to pay (I couldn't resist the pun). Ultimately, the only connection Set has to anything that might resemble evil is the land over which he governed, the desert. But it is Ra that keeps Set's home scorched. His battle with Osiris, Isis, and their son, Horus, was the type of drama that is associated with almost all of the deity forms. I've never heard of anyone complaining about Hera. Many goddess forms have a negative side, as do we all. But like Set, they are not the sum total of evil that Christian mythology says Satan is. Are we so desperate to fill the hole that was left when we stopped believing in Satan?

Associated Plant(s): myrrh, patchouli, thistle.

Associated Mineral(s): black diamond.

Associated Extracts and Concentration(s): *musk (oil), *civit (oil), myrrh (oil), patchouli (oil), thistle (tincture).

Shiva [Hindu]

Destruction, regeneration, evolution, dance, rhythm of the universe, self-sacrifice.

Another god form who is often thrown into the role of Satan. Very few people in the Wiccan community would have a thing to say about a woman using Kali (a form of his wife Parvati) as a role model. But what about her husband Shiva? Even though his name means "benevolent" or "favorable," he tends to be thrown into the category of black magick, as if there was such a thing.

When I was first introduced to the craft, I was told "For life, there must be death." Shiva is the god form that illustrates this principle. He is both the destroyer and regenerator. As destroyer, he is pictured with a necklace of skulls. Often, demons trot along behind him. But as the regenerator, he is the sacred life-giving phallus. This principle is marked by the naming of a sacred stone. He dances to the rhythm of the universe, both creative and destructive.

Shiva is change. To understand Shiva is to understand evolution. How far would the human race have evolved if not for survival of the fittest? We may have forgotten the simple natural law that Shiva represents, but the universe has not. Time and time again, it is made absolutely clear that "for life, there *must* be death."

Associated Plant(s): dragon's blood, geranium.

Associated Mineral(s): ruby, star ruby, turquoise.

Associated Concentrations and Extract(s): geranium (oil), *musk (oil), dragon's blood (perfume oil).

Shu [Egyptian]

Separation, air, opposing energy in balance.

Shu placed himself between the sky and the Earth to keep them separated. He is often depicted holding up Nuit (Nut), the sky goddess.

Associated Plant(s): damiana, jasmine.

Associated Mineral(s): quartz, lead.

Associated Extracts and Concentration(s): jasmine (absolute), damiana (tincture).

Silvanus [Roman]

Guardian of borders and limits.

One of the forgotten horned god forms. Silvanus is a god form of forests and uncultivated fields. Most people associate him with the Greek Silenus, but he does not seem to have the air of drunkenness that is inseparable from Silenus.

Associated Plant(s): pine, juniper.

Associated Concentrations and Extract(s): pine (oil), juniper berry (oil).

Associated Base Oil(s): olive oil.

Surya [Hindu]

Compromise, ordering priorities.

The most important message brought by Surya is to order priorities and compromise when need be. We can't always have exactly what we want and sometimes we have to compromise one area of our lives for the sake of another. Surya's wife left him because he was too bright. He convinced her to return by giving up a portion of his rays.

Associated Plant(s): frankincense, cinnamon, sandalwood, sunflower.

Associated Extracts and Concentrate(s): cinnamon (oil), frankincense (oil).

Associated Base Oil (s): sunflower oil.

Tane [Polynesian]

(May correspond to the Egyptian Shu.) New understanding, turning over a new leaf.

Tane wakes up early and goes to the eastern-most part of the horizon. There, he lifts the veil of night so that the universe can see the Earth and we can see part of the universe.

Associated Plant(s): kava-kava.

Thor [Norse]

(Possible correspondence to the Dagda.) Common man's god, strength, marriage, sexual stamina.

Now here is a god form Wiccans tend to hear about, but rarely spend any time with. Or do they? Thor is the common man's god, like the Dagda. His weapon (the hammer) is a huge blunt instrument, as is the Dagda's mighty club. One of the Dagda's titles was Ollathair (Father of All), and Thor's father, Odin, was often called the "All Father." Thor's mother has been listed several ways, but she is usually a giant. The Dagda was described as a giant himself. The Dagda is often described as being nourishing, and Thor is a god of the storms that nourish the earth. I think we are starting to see a trend here.

Associated Plant(s): American daisy, European daisy, gorse, nettle, oak, rowan, thistle), vervain.

Associated Mineral(s): ruby, iron, sulphur.

Associated Concentrations and Extract(s): nettle (tincture), white oak bark (tincture), thistle (tincture), vervain (tincture).

Thoth [Egyptian]

Wisdom, knowledge, literacy, science, justice, precision.

If the gods were to incorporate, Thoth would be the corporate secretary. He is the perfect recordkeeper or scribe. He is the god of the accountant. Invoke him at tax time and while balancing your checkbook, but don't expect anything but the truth to appear in those numbers. Thoth represents precision and truth.

Associated Plant(s): benzoin, vervain.

Associated Mineral(s): opal, fire opal, mercury.

Associated Extracts and Concentration(s): benzoin (tincture or oil), vervain (tincture).

Zeus [Greek]

Protector, provider, man of the household.

Zeus is a protector, especially of women who like to scheme. He was constantly trying to help those his wife Hera put at risk. He is also a rain god form, providing the water necessary to grow crops. Although he is not credited with the creation of humanity, he most certainly has adopted us, so we can feel comfortable thinking of him as a father figure.

Associated Plant(s): almond, damiana, fig, hyssop, jasmine, oak, poplar, saffron.

Associated Mineral(s): diamond, quartz, topaz, chalcedony, amethyst, lapis lazuli, lead.

Associated Concentrations and Extract(s): *ambergris (oil), jasmine (absolute), galbanum (oil).

Planetary associations

When we talk about planetary associations, we are neither discussing the planets themselves, nor any deity form that may bear the same name. When we refer to the sun as a planet, it does not negate our comprehension of the heliocentric orbit of the planets. But even though the sun and moon are not actually planets, they are planetary archetypes. As such, the names of each of the seven planetary archetypes are simply names given to patterns that have been observed. Earth and the outer planets are missing from the list because the patterns were named after heavenly bodies that could be observed at that time from Earth. They may have clear connections to the actual heavenly bodies that they are named after, but if such a link is ever proven, then these patterns will be more a matter of science than of magick.

Key = Name (common name) [day of week—gender*— primary color—element]—other associations

A few of the planetary associations can be presented either masculine or feminine. Where this occurs, I have had the greatest success associated them with the gender that most frequently aligns with the that pattern. Where such a situation has taken place, I have listed them with the association I have found to work best.

Sol (sun) [Sunday—masculine—yellow—Air]—Encourages a sense of authority, courage, creativity, and leadership that may lead to healing, victory in legal matters, advancement in employment, and atonement to masculine principles and male divinity.

Male Deity Association(s): Apollo (Greek), Dionysus (Greek), Ra (Egyptian), Helios (Greek), Sol (Roman), Shamash (Babylonian), Vishnu (Hindu).

Associated Plant(s): acacia, angelica, ash, bay, benzoin, carnation, cashew, cedar, celandine, chamomile, chicory, chrysanthemum, cinnamon, copal, eyebright, frankincense, goldenseal, gum arabic, gum mastic, hazel, heliotrope, juniper, lime, lovage, marigold, mistletoe, oak, olive, orange, palm, pineapple, rice, rosemary, rowan, rue, saffron, St. John's Wort, sesame, sunflower, tangerine, tea, walnut, witch hazel.

Associated Concentrations and Extract(s): bay (oil), benzoin (tincture or oil), bergamot (oil), cedar wood (oil), chamomile (oil), cinnamon (oil), copal (tincture), frankincense (oil), gum arabic (tincture), gum mastic (tincture), juniper berry (oil), lime (oil), neroli (oil), marigold (oil), orange (oil), rosemary (oil).

Associated Minerals: calcite (orange), carnelian, diamond, sunstone, tiger's eye, topaz.

Associated Base Oils: sunflower oil, sesame oil, olive oil.

Luna (Moon) [Monday—feminine—violet—Air]—Encourages a sense of thoughtful passion, intelligence, family, and a willingness to grow and change. Brings on dreams and assists in connectivity to the feminine principles and female divinity.

Male Deity Association(s): Khonsu (Egyptian), Sin (Babylonian), Shiva (Hindu), Varuna (Hindu).

Associated Plant(s): aloe, cabbage, calamus, camphor, chickweed, coconut, cotton, cucumber, eucalyptus, gardenia, gourd, grape, irish moss, jasmine, lemon, lettuce, lily, lotus, myrrh, papaya, poppy, potato, sandalwood, willow, wintergreen.

Associated Concentrations and Extract(s): camphor (oil), eucalyptus (oil), gardenia (absolute), jasmine (absolute), lemon (oil), myrrh (oil), sandalwood (oil).

Associated Mineral(s): aquamarine, beryl, moonstone, platinum, sapphire, silver.

Associated Base Oil: grapeseed oil.

Mars [Tuesday—masculine—red—Fire]—Encourages a sense of enthusiasm, physical strength, lust, and courage that may lead to protection during conflict, as well as conflict resolution. Although these attributes are typically thought of as only pertaining to figurative wars, this archetype definitely pertains to the infliction of death that is necessary during both war and hunting situations.

Male Deity Association: Agni (Hindu), Ares (Greek), Horus (Egyptian), Mars (Roman), Maris (Etruscan), Ninurta (Babylonian), Nusku (Babylonian).

Associated Plant(s): allspice, asafetida, ash, bamboo, basil, bloodroot, broom, chili pepper, coriander, cubeb, cumin, damiana, dragon's blood, galangal, ginger, high john, holly, hops, horseradish, leek, mustard, nettle, onion, pennyroyal, pepper, peppermint, pimento, pine, radish, rowan, sloe, snapdragon, thistle, woodruff, wormwood.

Associated Concentrations and Extract(s): basil (oil), allspice (oil), coriander (oil), dragon's blood (perfume oil), peppermint (oil), pine (oil).

Associated Mineral(s): agate (red), bloodstone, flint, garnet, iron, jasper (red), lava, nickel, onyx, rhodocrosite, rhodonite, ruby, sard, sardonyx, tourmaline (red).

Associated Base Oil(s): Olive Oil and Coconut Oil

Mercury [Wednesday—masculine—yellow—Water]— Encourages learning, divisiveness, intelligence, communication skills, and may improve divination, teaching skills, and dedication. Secures against doubt, tiring, and exhaustion.

Male Deity Association(s): Cilans (Etruscan), Ganesha (Hindu), Hermes (Greek), Mercury (Roman), Nabu (Babylonian), Thoth (Egyptian), Turms (Etruscan).

Associated Plants : almond, angelica, bean, benzoin, brazil nut, caraway, celery, clove, clover, dill, fennel, fenugreek, flax, gum arabic, gum mastic, horehound, lavender, lemongrass, lemon verbena, mace, marjoram, mint, mulberry, orange, papyrus, parsley, peppermint, pistachio, pomegranate, star anise.

Associated Extracts and Concentrations: benzoin (tincture or oil), bergamot (oil), clove (oil), gum arabic (tincture), gum mastic (tincture), lavender (oil), lemongrass (oil), orange (oil), peppermint (oil).

Associated Minerals: agate (banded), aventurine, carnelian, fire opal, jasper (mottled), mica, pumice.

Associated Base Oil: almond oil.

Jupiter [Thursday—masculine—blue—Water]—Brings confidence in matters of finance and tangible property. This may aid in luck in gambling and with matters of the law.

Male Deity Associations: Zeus (Greek), Poseidon (Greek), Iuppiter (Roman), Tina (Etruscan), Marduk (Babylonian), Indra (Hindu), Hapi (Egyptian).

Associated Plants: anise, borage, cedar, chestnut, chinquefoil, clove, dandelion, fig, flax, honeysuckle, hyssop, juniper, lime, maple, nutmeg, oak, oakmoss, olive, pine, sage, sassafras, sarsaparilla, star anise.

Associated Extracts and Concentrations: clove (oil), cedar wood (oil), nutmeg (oil), juniper (oil), lime (oil), pine (oil), sage (oil).

Associated Minerals: aquamarine, amethyst, antimony, labradorite, lapis lazuli, lepidolite, sapphire, sugilite, tin, turquoise, zinc.

Associated Base Oils: olive oil.

Venus [Friday—feminine—green—Fire]—attracting love and strengthening partnerships/unions, pleasure, creativity in all arts especially music.

Male Deity Associations: none.

Associated Plants: adam and eve, apricot, banana, barley, buckwheat, coltsfoot, corn, daffodil, daisy, dittany of crete, elder, feverfew, fig, geranium (rose), hawthorn, heather, hibiscus, huckleberry, hyacinth, iris, lady's mantle, lemon, lemon verbena, licorice, lilac, lime, magnolia, mugwort, myrtle, oats, orange, orris, passion flower, pea, peach, pear, periwinkle, plum, raspberry, rhubarb, rose (red), rye, santal, spearmint, spikenard, strawberry, suger cane, tansy, thyme, tulip, tonka, valerian, vanilla, vervain, vetivert, violet, wheat, willow, wood aloes, ylang-ylang.

Associated Extracts and Concentrations: bergamot (oil), rose geranium (oil), lemon (oil), licorice (tincture), rose (oil), spearmint (oil), sweet orange (oil), vanilla (tincture), ylang-ylang (absolute).

Associated Minerals: amazonite, azurite, bronze, calcite (blue, green, pink), chrysoprase, copper, emerald, jade (green, pink, white), jasper (green), kunzite, lapis lazuli, malachite, olivine, peridot, salt (sea), sandstone, sodalite, tourmaline (blue, green, pink, watermelon), turquoise.

Associated Base Oil: Apricot Kernel Oil

Saturn [Saturday—feminine—indigo—Earth]—promotes and smooths transitions such as divorce, funerals, death, and reincarnation.

Male Deity Associations: Brahma (Hindu), Kronos (Greek), Ptah (Egyptian), Saeturnus (Roman), Ea (Babylonian), Shiva (Hindu).

Associated Plants: beech, beet, boneset, buckthorn, comfrey, cypress, elm, kava-kava, lady's slipper, lobelia, morning glory, mullein, myrrh, patchouli, pansy, poplar, scullcap, slippery elm, Solomon's seal, tamarind, spikenard, violet, yew.

Associated Extracts and Concentrations: cypress (oil), myrrh (oil), patchouli (oil).

Associated Minerals: apache tear, coal, hematite, jasper (brown), jet, obsidian, onyx, salt (especially black), tourmaline (black).

Associated Base Oils: none.

Astrological sign associations

Key = Sign (start date—end date) [ruling planet—element—associated colors]

The exact beginning and ending date for each sign will vary depending on the reference you choose. This is because the signs do not switch exactly at midnight. If you know the time of a person's birth and location, any reputable astrologer can give you that person's sun sign.

Aquarius (Jan. 20—Feb. 18) [Saturn/Uranus—Air—Blue and green]

Associated Plants: acacia, almond, benzoin, cypress, gum mastic, hops, lavender, lemon verbena, mace, parsley, patchouli, peppermint, pine, star anise.

Associated Extracts and concentrations: benzoin (tincture or oil), cypress (oil), gum mastic (tincture), lavender (oil), patchouli (oil), peppermint (oil), pine (oil).

Associated Minerals: aquamarine, garnet, jet, turquoise, hawkeye.

Associated Base Oils: almond oil.

Aries (Mar. 21—Apr. 19) [Mars—Fire—Pink, red, and white]

Associated Plants: allspice, black pepper, carnation, cedar, cinnamon, clove, copal, coriander, cumin, dragon's blood, fennel, frankincense, galangal, ginger, juniper, orange, pennyroyal, peppermint, pine, woodruff.

Associated Extracts and Concentrations: allspice berry (oil), black pepper (oil), cedar wood (oil), cinnamon (oil), clove (oil), copal (tincture), coriander seed (oil), cumin seed (oil), dragon's blood (perfume oil), fennel seed (oil), frankincense (oil), juniper berry (oil) *musk (oil), neroli (oil), petitgrain (oil), peppermint (oil).

Associated Minerals: bloodstone, carnelian, garnet, jasper (red), ruby.

Associated Base Oils: none.

Cancer (June 21—July 22) [Moon—Water—Brown, green, and white]

Associated Plants: calamus, chamomile, cardamom, eucalyptus, gardenia, jasmine, lemon, lily, lemon balm, lilac, lotus, myrrh, rose, sandalwood, violet, yarrow.

Associated Extracts and Concentrations: *ambergris (oil), chamomile (absolute), eucalyptus (oil), jasmine (absolute), lemon (oil), myrrh (oil), palmarosa (oil), rose (oil), sandalwood (oil).

Associated Minerals: beryl, chrysoprase, green adventurine, emerald, moonstone, sapphire.

Associated Base Oils: coconut oil.

Capricorn (Dec. 22—Jan. 19) [Saturn—Earth—Black, brown, and red]

Associated Plants: cypress, honeysuckle, lilac, magnolia, myrrh, oakmoss, patchouli, tonka, tulip, vervain, vetivert.

Associated Extracts and Concentrations: cypress (oil), myrrh (oil), patchouli (oil).

Associated Minerals: apache tear, cat's eye, hematite, onyx, ruby.

Associated Base Oils: none.

Gemini (May 21—June 20) [Mercury—Air—Blue, red, and yellow]

Associated Plants: almond, anise, benzoin, caraway, clover, dill, gum mastic, horehound, lavender, lemongrass, lily, mace, parsley, peppermint.

Associated Extracts and Concentrations: benzoin (absolute or tincture), gum mastic (tincture), lavender (oil), lemongrass (oil), peppermint (oil).

Associated Minerals: agate, aventurine, citrine, tiger's eye.

Associated Base Oils: almond oil.

Leo (July 23—Aug. 22) [Sun—Fire—Green, red, and yellow]

Associated Plants: acacia, bay, basil, benzoin, cinnamon, copal, frankincense, ginger, juniper, lime, nutmeg, orange, rosemary, sandalwood.

Associated Extracts and Concentrations: bay (oil), basil (oil), benzoin (tincture or oil), cinnamon (oil), copal (tincture), frankincense (oil), ginger (oil), juniper berry (oil), lime (oil), nutmeg (oil), musk* (oil), neroli (oil), orange (oil), petitgrain (oil), rosemary (oil), sandalwood (oil).

Associated Minerals: carnelian, citrine, diamond, onyx, quartz crystal, topaz.

Associated Base Oils: sunflower oil.

Libra (Sept. 23—Oct. 22) [Venus—Air—Black, blue, and yellow]

Associated Plants: catnip, chamomile, daffodil, dill, eucalyptus, fennel, geranium, lilac, marjoram, mugwort, peppermint, pine, rose, spearmint, thyme, vanilla, violet.

Associated Extracts and Concentrations: chamomile (absolute), eucalyptus (oil), fennel seed (oil), geranium (oil), palmarosa (oil), peppermint (oil), pine (oil), rose (oil), spearmint (oil), thyme (oil), vanilla (tincture).

Associated Minerals: chrysoprase, citrine, chrysolite, lapis lazuli, smokey quartz, turquoise.

Associated Base Oils: apricot kernel oil.

Pisces (Feb. 19—Mar. 20) [Jupiter / Neptune—Water—Green and white]

Associated Plants: anise, apple, calamus, camphor, cardamom, catnip, clove, eucalyptus, gardenia, honeysuckle, hyacinth, jasmine, lemon, lilly, mugwort, myrrh, nutmeg, orris, sage, sandalwood, sarsaparilla, star anise, vanilla.

Associated Extracts and Concentrations: camphor (oil), cardamom (oil), clove (oil), eucalyptus (oil), jasmine (absolute), lemon (oil), myrrh (oil), nutmeg (oil), sage (oil), sandalwood (oil), palmarosa (oil), vanilla (tincture), ylang-ylang (absolute).

Associated Minerals: amethyst, sugilite.

Associated Base Oils: none.

Sagittarius (Nov. 22—Dec. 21) [Jupiter—Fire—Purple, red, and yellow]

Associated Plants: anise, calendula, carnation, cedar, clove, copal, deerstongue, dragon's blood, frankincense, ginger, honeysuckle, hyssop, juniper, lemon balm, mace, nutmeg, oakmoss, orange, rose, rosemary, saffron, sage, sassafras, star anise.

Associated Extracts and Concentrations: anise seed (oil), bergamot (oil), cedar wood (oil), clove (oil), copal (tincture), dragon's blood (perfume oil), frankincense (oil), ginger (oil), juniper berry (oil), nutmeg (oil), orange (oil), petigrain (oil), rose (oil), rosemary (oil), sage (oil).

Associated Minerals: amethyst, chalcedony, sugilite, topaz.

Associated Base Oils: none.

Scorpio (Oct. 23—Nov. 21) [Mars—Water—Black, brown, and red]

Associated Plants: allspice, basil, black pepper, cardamom, clove, coffee, cumin, galangal, gardenia, ginger, hyacinth, hops, myrrh, pennyroyal, pine, thyme, vanilla, violet, woodruff.

Associated Extracts and Concentrations: allspice (oil), ambergris* (oil), basil (oil), black pepper (oil), cardamom seed (oil), clove (oil), cumin seed (oil), ginger (oil), myrrh (oil), pine (oil), thyme (oil), vanilla (tincture).

Associated Minerals: aquamarine, carnelian (red), kunzite, spinel, tourmalated quartz crystal.

Associated Base Oils: none.

Taurus (Apr. 20—May 20) [Venus—Earth—Green, red, and yellow]

Associated Plants: apple, cardamom, daisy, honeysuckle, lilac, magnolia, oakmoss, patchouli, rose, thyme, tonka, vanilla, violet.

Associated Extracts and Concentrations: cardamom seed (oil), patchouli (oil), rose (oil), thyme (oil), vanilla (tincture), ylang-ylang (absolute).

Associated Minerals: emerald, jade, lapis lazuli, sapphire, quartz (rose).

Associated Base Oils: apricot kernel.

Virgo (Aug. 23—Sept. 22) [Mercury—Earth—Black, gray, and yellow]

Associated Plants: almond, caraway, cypress, dill, fennel, honeysuckle, lavender, lemon balm, lily, mace, moss, oakmoss, patchouli, peppermint.

Associated Extracts and Concentrations: cypress (oil), fennel seed (oil), lavender (oil), patchouli (oil), peppermint (oil).

Associated Minerals: agate, aventurine, citrine, carnelian.

Associated Base Oils: almond oil.

Elemental associations

In the same way the Earth is not listed as a planet because it is the point from where the reference is made to the other planets, Akasha (the fifth element) is not listed here because it is the point of reference from which the other elements are considered.

Key = Name (gender—bodily element) [direction—primary color]—other associations

Earth (feminine—body) [North—green]—Encourages peaceful grounding or centering and thus promotes a sense of stability. With this good foundation, this pattern may help you build money and business success. For obvious reasons, this element is also associated with gardening, agriculture, and the fertility of the Earth. Of all the elements, Earth provides the least permeable state and should not be used when change is desired.

Associated Plants: alfalfa, barley, beet, corn, cotton, cypress, lilac, magnolia, mugwort, oats, patchouli, pea, potato, primrose, rhubarb, rye, tonka, tulip, turnip, vervain, vetivert, wheat.

Associated Extracts and Concentrations: cypress (oil), patchouli (oil).

Associated Minerals: agate (green or moss), alum, calcite (green), chrysoprase, emerald, jasper (brown and green), jet, kunzite, malachite, olivine, peridot, salt (rock), tourmaline (black and green), turquoise.

Associated Base Oils: none.

Air (masculine—breath) [East—yellow]—Encourages exchange and the welcome of new information, hence, it is the element of communication, travel, and the intellect. May also be associated with harmony in relationships of the heart, as lack of communication is often the downfall of an otherwise stable relationship. Air promotes gradual change.

Associated Plants: acacia, almond, anise, bean, benzoin, brazil nut, broom, caraway, celery, chicory, clover, dandelion, dill, eyebright, fennel, fenugreek, gum mastic, hazel, hops, lavender, lemongrass, lemon verbena, lily of the valley, mace, maple, marjoram, mint, mulberry, palm, papyrus, parsley, pecan, pine, pistachio, rice, sage, star anise.

Associated Extracts and Concentrations: benzoin (tincture or oil), fennel seed (oil), gum mastic (tincture), lavender (oil), lemongrass (oil), niaouli (oil), pine (oil), sage (oil).

Associated Minerals: aventurine, jasper (mottled), mica, pumice, sphene.

Associated Base Oils: almond oil, palm oil.

Fire (masculine—spirit) [South—red]—Fire is the element of purification and sudden change. As such, it also encourages growth. Where we might feel the urge to leap back from this element, there are certain plants that absolutely will not grow unless their seed husk is broken in forest fires. It is associated with both strong defensive and offensive magick; however, you should be very careful when working with this element because it can get out of control very easily.

Associated Plants: allspice, angelica, asafetida, ash, basil, bay, bloodroot, broom, cactus, carnation, carrot, cashew, cedar, celandine, celery, chestnut, chili pepper, chrysanthemum, cinnamon, cinquefoil, clove, coffee, copal, coriander, cubeb, cumin, curry, damiana, dill, dragon's blood, fennel, fig, flax, frankincense, galangal, garlic, ginger, hawthorn, high john, hyssop, juniper, lime, lovage, marigold, mustard, nutmeg, oak, olive, onion, orange, pennyroyal, pepper, peppermint, pimento, pineapple, pomegranate, radish, rosemary, rowan, rue, saffron, St. John's Wort, sarsaparilla, sassafras, sesame, sloe, snapdragon, sunflower, tangerine, tea, thistle, walnut, witch hazel, woodruff, wormwood.

Associated Extracts and Concentrations: allspice (oil), basil (oil), bay (oil), bergamot (oil), black pepper (oil), cedar wood (oil), cinnamon (oil), clove (oil), copal (tincture), coriander (oil), dragon's blood (perfume oil), frankincense (oil), ginger (oil), juniper berry (oil), lime (oil), neroli (oil), nutmeg (oil), orange (oil), rosemary (oil).

Associated Minerals: agate (banded, black, brown, and red), apache tear, bloodstone, carnelian, citrine, diamond, flint, garnet, hematite, jasper (red), lava, obsidian, onyx, rhodocrosite, ruby, sard, sardonyx, serpentine, spinel, sunstone, tiger's-eye, topaz, tourmaline (red).

Associated Base Oils: olive oil, sunflower oil.

Water (feminine—blood) [West—blue]—Brings on sleep, rest, peace, and prophecy. Water does cause change, but not nearly as abruptly as Fire. This is why it is used in rituals for healing, love, compassion, and other intents where gentle change is needed. Like Fire, it is a cleansing element. It is used in preparations for purification when subtle force is desired. Like Earth, Water is an anti-stressing element, but Water is the element to choose for an event, where Earth is used for more of an ongoing practice.

Associated Plants: adam and eve, aloe, apple, apricot, avocado, balm of gilead, banana, birch, blackberry, bladderwrack, boneset, buckthorn, cabbage, calamus, camphor, cardamom, catnip, cherry, chickweed, coconut, coltsfoot, comfrey, cucumber, daisy, dittany of crete, elder, elm, eucalyptus, feverfew, foxglove, gardenia, geranium, gourd, grape, heather, hibiscus, huckleberry, hyacinth, iris, irish moss, jasmine, kava kava, lady's mantle, lady's slipper, lemon, lettuce, licorice, lilac, lily, lobelia, lotus, magnolia, morning glory, mugwort, myrrh, orris, pansy, papaya, passion flower, peach, pear, periwinkle, plum, poplar, poppy, raspberry, rose, sandalwood, scullcap, Solomon's seal, spearmint, spikenard, strawberry, sugar cane, tamarind, tamarisk, tansy, thyme, tomato, tonka, valerian, vanilla, violet, willow, wintergreen, yarrow.

Associated Extracts and Concentrations: camphor (oil), cardamom (oil), eucalyptus (oil), jasmine (absolute), lemon (oil), myrrh (oil), rose (oil), sandalwood (oil), thyme (oil), vanilla (tincture), ylang-ylang (oil).

Associated Minerals: agate (blue lace), amethyst, aquamarine, azurite, beryl, calcite (blue and pink), celestite, chalcedony, chrysocolla, jade, lapis lazuli, moonstone, sapphire, selenite, sodalite, sugilite, tourmaline (blue, green, and pink).

Associated Base Oils: apricot kernel oil, coconut oil, grapeseed oil.

Color associations

Key = Color (diatonic scale value) [astrological signs]

Red (C) [Aries, Scorpio]

Associated Extracts and Concentrations: frankincense, myrrh, patchouli, vetiver.

Associated Mineral: quartz (smokey), tourmaline (black and red), garnet.

Associated with: the root chakra, or muladhara, at the base of the spine, and thus associated with the health of the blood circulation system and testicles.

Associated emotional response: increases anger, lust, fear, sense of health, confidence, and strength. Causes general irritation with long-term exposure.

Orange (D) [Leo]

Associated Extracts and Concentrations: jasmine (absolute), rose (oil), sandalwood (oil), ylang-ylang (oil).

Associated Minerals: garnet, topaz (imperial), tourmaline (red), rose quartz (especially in the crystal form).

Associated with: the sacral chakra and thus with the health of the genitalia and the urinary system.

Associated emotional response: encourages thought and contemplation, opens the mind to new ideas, willingness to change, and a general feeling of fulfillment.

Yellow (E) [Taurus, Libra]

Associated Extracts and Concentrations: basil (oil), clary sage (oil), lemon (oil), neroli (oil).

Associated Minerals: beryl (golden), citrine, tourmaline (green and pink).

Associated with: the solar plexus chakra and thus with the health of the digestive system, spleen, stomach, liver, pancreas, and adrenal glands.

Associated emotional response: brings on jealousy, happiness, confidence, and a general sense of well-being. Yellow is an excellent color to use in retail sales or other situations where you seek to persuade.

Green (F) [Cancer]

Associated Extracts and Concentrates: bergamot (oil), geranium (oil), rose (oil), neroli (oil).

Associated Minerals: emerald, tourmaline (green and pink), rose quarts (especially crystals).

Associated with: the heart chakra and thus with the health of the circulatory system and thymus gland.

Associated emotional response: brings on a willingness to receive (especially pleasure), causes a general feeling of mental energy, encourages growth and willingness to nurture.

Blue (G) [Capricorn, Sagittarius]

Associated Extracts and Concentrates: camphor (oil), chamomile (absolute), neroli (oil).

Associated Minerals: aquamarine, tourmaline (blue), silver.

Associated with: the throat chakra and thus with the health of the respiratory system, lungs, and thyroid gland.

Associated emotional response: encourages a feeling of peace and calm, brings on relaxation, patience, emotional honesty, and a general feeling of good health.

Indigo (A) [Aquarius, Pisces]

Associated Extracts and Concentrates: lavender (oil), rosemary (oil).

Associated Minerals: amethyst, sapphire, tourmaline.

Associated with: the third eye chakra and thus with the health of the nervous system, lower brain, sight, hearing, and pituitary gland.

Associated emotional response: increased ambition and the willingness to change to reach ambitious goals.

Violet (B) [Gemini, Virgo]

Associated Extracts and Concentrations: frankincense (oil), jasmine (absolute), lavender (oil), sandalwood (oil).

Associated Minerals: amethyst, diamond, gold.

Associated with: the crown chakra and thus the central nervous system, upper brain, and pineal gland.

Associated emotional response: brings on a sense of empowerment.

Associations of specific intents

Key = Intent, Specification [gender]

Astral Travel and Etheric Change, to enable

Associated Plants: benzoin, cinnamon, jasmine, mugwort, poplar, sandalwood.

Associated Extracts and Concentrations: benzoin (oil and tincture), cinnamon (oil), jasmine (absolute), sandalwood (oil).

Associated Minerals: opal, tourmalated quartz crystal.

Associated Base Oil: none.

Banishing, forcing out that which is not desired

Associated Plants: angelica, asafetida, basil, beans, birch, boneset, buckthorn, cayenne pepper, clove, clover, coal, cumin, dragon's blood, elder, fern, frankincense, garlic, heliotrope, horehound, horseradish, juniper, leek, lilac, mint, mullein, myrrh, nettle, onion, peach, peony, peppermint, pine, rosemary, rue, sandalwood, sloe, snapdragon, tamarisk, thistle, vetivert, yarrow.

Associated Extracts and Concentrations: basil (oil), clove (oil), cumin seed (oil), dragon's blood (perfume oil), frankincense (oil), juniper berry (oil), myrrh (oil), peppermint (oil), pine (oil), rosemary (oil), sandalwood (oil).

Associated Minerals: pumice, salt (rock and sea), sulfur.

Associated Base Oil: none.

Celibacy, to strengthen conviction to

Associated Plants: camphor, lavender, and marjoram.

Associated Extracts and Concentrations: camphor (oil), lavender.

Associated Minerals: none.

Associated Base Oils: none.

Cognitive Abilities, to stimulate the thought process of the conscious mind

Associated Plants: basil, bay, black pepper, caraway, coffee, dill, honeysuckle, hyssop, lavender, lilac, lily of the valley, pennyroyal, peppermint, rosemary, rue, saffron, sage, thyme.

Associated Extracts and Concentrations: basil (oil), bay (oil), black pepper (oil), lavender (oil), peppermint (oil), rosemary (oil).

Associated Minerals: aventurine, emerald, fluorite, sphene.

Associated Base Oil: none.

Courage and Bravery, to promote a sense of

Associated Plants: allspice, black pepper, cedar, clove, dragon's blood, fennel, frankincense, geranium (rose), ginger, mullein, onion, tea, thyme, tonka, yarrow.

Associated Extracts and Concentrations: allspice berry (oil), black pepper (oil), cedar wood (oil), clove (oil), dragon's blood (perfume oil), fennel seed (oil), frankincense (oil), ginger (oil), musk* (oil), rose geranium (oil).

Associated Minerals: agate, amethyst, aquamarine, bloodstone, carnelian, diamond, lapis lazuli, sard, sardonyx, tiger's eye, tourmaline (red), turquoise.

Associated Base Oil: none.

Defense/Protection

Associated Plants: cypress, myrrh, patchouli, geranium (rose), rosemary, rue, violet.

Associated Extracts and Concentrations: lava, onyx, sapphire.

Associated Minerals: cypress (oil), myrrh (oil), patchouli (oil), rose geranium (oil), rosemary (oil).

Associated Base Oil: none.

Depression, to decrease

Associated Plants: basil, jasmine, lemon balm, sage.

Associated Extracts and Concentrations: basil (oil), jasmine (absolute), sage (oil), ylang-ylang (absolute).

Associated Minerals: amethyst, chrysoprase.

Associated Base Oil: none.

Divination/Acquisition of Etheric Knowledge of the Future

Associated Plants: anise, broom camphor, calendula, camphor, clove, cherry, cinquefoil, dandelion, fig, goldenrod, hibiscus, jasmine, marigold, meadowsweet, mugwort, orange, orris, pomegranate, rose.

Associated Extracts and Concentrations: bergamot (oil), camphor (oil), clove (oil), jasmine (absolute), orange (oil), petitgrain (oil), rose (oil).

Associated Minerals: Azurite, flint, hematite, jet, mica, moonstone, obsidian, tiger's eye.

Associated Base Oil: none.

Dreams, to promote

Associated Plants: lavender, sage, vervain.

Associated Extracts and Concentrations: lavender (oil), sage (oil).

Associated Minerals: amethyst, azurite, citrine.

Associated Base Oil: none.

Energy (physical), to encourage a sense of

Associated Plants: bay, black pepper, camphor, caraway, carnation, cinnamon, garlic, ginger, lemon, lime, nutmeg, orange, patchouli, pennyroyal, pine, saffron, vanilla.

Associated Extracts and Concentrations: bay (oil), bergamot (oil), black pepper (oil), camphor (oil), cinnamon (oil), garlic (oil), lemon (oil), orange (oil), patchouli (oil), peppermint (oil), petigrain (oil), pine (oil), vanilla (tincture).

Associated Minerals: calcite, rhodocrosite, selinite, sunstone, tiger's eye, tourmaline (red).

Associated Base Oil: none.

Friendship, to encourage

Associated Plants: lemon, orange, passion flower.

Associated Extracts and Concentrations: bergamot (oil), lemon (oil), orange (oil), petitgrain (oil).

Associated Minerals: chrysoprase, tourmaline (pink), turquoise (when given as a gift).

Associated Base Oil: none.

Grounding/Anti-stress/Centering

Associated Plants: benzoin, cumin, gardenia, hyacinth, magnolia, rose.

Associated Extracts and Concentrations: benzoin (tincture and oil), cumin seed (oil), rose (oil).

Associated Minerals: calcite, hematite, kunzite, moonstone, obsidian, salt, tourmaline (black).

Associated Base Oil: none.

Happiness, to promote

Associated Plants: apple, basil, catnip, celandine, hawthorn, high john, hyacinth, lavender, lily of the valley, marjoram, morning glory, orange, saffron, sesame, St. John's Wort.

Associated Extracts and Concentrations: bergamot (oil), basil (oil), lavender (oil), neroli (oil), petitgrain (oil).

Associated Minerals: amethyst, chrysoprase.

Associated Base Oil: none.

Hex and Curse Breaking, to rid another person's influence

Associated Plants: chili pepper, frankincense, galangal, huckleberry, hydrangea, sage, thistle, vetivert, wintergreen.

Associated Extracts and Concentrations: frankincense (oil), sage (oil), wintergreen (oil).

Associated Minerals: salt (rock and sea), sulfur.

Associated Base Oil: none.

Healing, to encourage a mental image of health

Associated Plants: allspice, angelica, apple, balm of gilead, barley, bay, blackberry, burdock, carnation, cedar, cinnamon, coriander, cucumber, cypress, elder, eucalyptus, fennel, flax, gardenia, garlic, ginseng, golden seal, heliotrope, henna, hops, horehound, ivy, jobe's tears, lemon balm, lime, lotus, melon (especially water melon), mint, mugwort, myrrh, nettle, oak, olive, onion, peppermint, pine, potato, rose, rosemary, rowan, saffron, sandalwood, spearmint, thistle, thyme, vervain, violet, willow, wintergreen.

Associated Extracts and Concentrations: allspice berry (oil), bay (oil), cedar wood (oil), cinnamon (oil), coriander seed (oil), cypress (oil), eucalyptus (oil), myrrh (oil), niaouli (oil), palmarosa (oil), peppermint (oil), rose (oil), rosemary (oil), sandalwood (oil), spearmint (oil), wintergreen (oil).

Associated Minerals: agate (blue lace, green, and moss), amethyst, azurite, calcite (blue, green, pink), celestite, chrysoprase, jade, jasper (brown and green), jet, lapis lazuli, peridot, petrified wood, sapphire, sodalite, sugilite, turquoise.

Associated Base Oil: olive.

Health, to maintain

Associated Plants: ash, camphor, caraway, carnation, coriander, eucalyptus, garlic, galangal, geranium, juniper, lavender, lemon, marjoram, melon, mullein, nutmeg, oak, pine, St. John's Wort, sandalwood, sassafras, spikenard, tansy, thyme, walnut.

Associated Extracts and Concentrations: camphor (oil), coriander seed (oil), eucalyptus (oil), juniper berry (oil), lavender (oil), lemon (oil), pine (oil), sandalwood (oil), thyme (oil).

Associated Minerals: agate (banded, black, brown, and red), aventurine, bloodstone, calcite (orange), carnelian, diamond, flint, garnet, hematite, jasper (mottled and red), staurolite, sunstone, topaz.

Associated Base Oil: none.

Love, to inspire love in a woman [feminine]

Associated Plants: adam and eve, apple, apricot, avocado, balm of gilead, barley, beet, cardamom, cherry, chickweed, coltsfoot, daffodil, daisy, elm, gardenia, hibiscus, hyacinth, iris, jasmine, kava-kava, lady's mantle, lemon, licorice, lilac, lobelia, lotus, myrtle, nutmeg, orris, pansy, peach, peppermint, plum, poppy, primrose, raspberry, rose, rye, scullcap, spearmint, strawberry, sugar cane, tamarind, thyme, tomato, tonka, tulip, valerian, vetivert, violet, willow, yarrow.

Associated Extracts and Concentrations: cardamom seed (oil), jasmine (absolute), lemon (oil), nutmeg (oil), peppermint (oil), rose (oil), spearmint (oil).

Associated Minerals: agate (blue lace, green, and moss), amethyst, beryl, calcite (blue, green, and pink), chrysocolla, emerald, jade, lapis lazuli, malachite, moonstone, olivine, sapphire, tourmaline (pink), turquoise.

Associated Base Oil: apricot kernel oil.

Love, to encourage a male to have a mental image of being loved [masculine]

Associated Plants: basil, beans, bloodroot, chili pepper, clove, clover, copal, coriander, cubeb, damiana, dill, dragon's blood, fig, ginger, gum mastic, high john, juniper, lavender, lemon verbena, lime, lovage, maple, marjoram, orange, peppermint, pimento, rosemary, saffron, sarsaparilla, vanilla, wormwood.

Associated Extracts and Concentrations: basil (oil), clove (oil), copal (tincture), coriander seed (oil), dragon's blood (perfume oil), gum mastic (oil), juniper berry (oil), lavender (oil), lime (oil), orange (oil), peppermint (oil), rosemary (oil).

Associated Minerals: agate (banded, black, brown, and especially red), alexandrite, calcite (orange), lepidolite, rhodocrosite, sard, topaz.

Associated Base Oil: none.

Luck, to encourage a sense of

Associated Plants: allspice, calamus, hazel, heather, irish moss, nutmeg, orange, poppy seed, rose, spikenard, star anise, tonka, vetivert, violet.

Associated Extracts and Concentrations: allspice berry (oil), bergamot (oil), orange (oil), petitgrain (oil), rose (oil).

Associated Minerals: alexandrite, apache tear, aventurine, chalcedony, chrysoprase, cross stone, jet, lepidolite, olivine, opal, sardonyx, tiger's-eye, turquoise (when given or received as a gift).

Associated Base Oil: none.

Lust, to encourage a sense of lust in a woman for a man [feminine]

Associated Plants: bay, cardamom, kava-kava, patchouli, rose, sandalwood, vetivert, violet.

Associated Extracts and Concentrations: bay (oil), cardamom seed (oil), civit* (oil), musk* (oil), patchouli (oil), rose (oil), sandalwood (oil).

Associated Minerals: carnelian, rose quartz, tourmaline (green).

Associated Base Oil: none.

Lust, to encourage a sense of lust in a man for a woman [masculine]

Associated Plants: vanilla, gardenia, ginger, jasmine, lavender, nutmeg, yohimbe.

Associated Extracts and Concentrations: ginger (oil), jasmine (absolute), neroli (oil), nutmeg (oil).

Associated Minerals: chrysoprase, moonstone, rhodochrosite.

Associated Base Oil: none.

Meditation and Focus on Intent

Associated Plants: acacia, chamomile, frankincense, hyacinth, jasmine, magnolia, myrrh, nutmeg, sandalwood.

Associated Extracts and Concentrations: chamomile (absolute), frankincense (oil), jasmine (absolute), myrrh (oil), sandalwood (oil).

Associated Minerals: sapphire, sodalite.

Associated Base Oil: none.

Memory, to stimulate the portions of the brain responsible for

Associated Plants: clove, coriander, lily of the valley, rosemary, sage.

Associated Extracts and Concentrations: clove (oil), coriander seed (oil), rosemary (oil), sage (oil).

Associated Minerals: quartz crystal (clear).

Associated Base Oil: none.

Nightmares, to end the distraction of

Associated Plants: lavender, chamomile, rosemary.

Associated Extracts and Concentrations: lavender (oil), rosemary (oil).

Associated Minerals: chalcedony, citrine, jet, lepidolite, ruby.

Associated Base Oil: none.

Protection, to promote a sense of protection and well-being

Associated Plants: angelica, anise, asafetida, balm of gilead, basil, bay, black pepper, broom, calamus, caraway, carnation, cedar, cinnamon, cinquefoil, clove, clover, copal, cumin, cypress, dill, dragon's blood, eucalyptus, fennel, flax, frankincense, galangal, garlic, geranium (rose), gum arabic, heather, honeysuckle, hyacinth, hyssop, juniper, lavender, lilac, lime, lotus, mugwort, myrrh, onion, orris, parsley, patchouli, peppermint, pennyroyal, pine, rose, rosemary, rue, sage, sandalwood, thistle, valerian, vervain, vetivert, violet, wisteria, wood aloe, woodruff, wormwood.

Associated Extracts and Concentrations: basil (oil), black pepper (oil), cedar wood (oil), cinnamon (oil), clove (oil), copal (tincture), cypress (oil), dragon's blood (perfume), juniper berry (oil), lavender (oil), lime (oil), myrrh (oil), niaouli (oil), pine (oil), rose (oil), rosemary (oil), sage (oil), sandalwood (oil).

Associated Minerals: agate, apache tear, calcite, carnelian, chalcedony, chrysoprase, citrine, diamond, emerald, flint, garnet, jade, jasper, jet, lapis lazuli, lava, lepidolite, malachite, mica, mooonstone, obsidian, olivine, onyx, peridot, pumice, ruby, salt (rock), sard, sardonyx, serpentine, staurolite, sunstone, tiger's-eye, topaz, tourmaline (black and red), turquoise (when received as a gift).

Associated Base Oil: olive oil.

Psychic abilities/Acquisition of Etheric Knowledge of the Present and Past (see also Divination)

Associated Plants: anise, bay, camphor, celery, cinnamon, clove, flax, galangal, gardenia, gum arabic, gum mastic, iris, honeysuckle, lemongrass, lilac, mace, marigold, mugwort, nutmeg, orange, orris, peppermint, rose, saffron, star anise, thyme, wormwood, yarrow.

Associated Extracts and Concentrations: bay (oil), bergamont (oil), camphor (oil), cinnamon (oil), gum arabic (tincture), gum mastic (tincture), lemongrass (oil), nutmeg (oil), orange (oil), petitgrain (oil), peppermint (oil), rose (oil), thyme (oil).

Associated Minerals: Amethyst, aquamarine, azurite, beryl, citrine, emerald, lapis lazuli.

Associated Base Oil: none.

Physical Strength, to bring a sense of

Associated Plants: acacia, anise, cassia, heliotrope, lemongrass, lilac, mimosa, nutmeg, sandalwood.

Associated Extracts and Concentrations: anise (tincture), lemongrass (oil), nutmeg (oil), sandalwood (oil).

Associated Minerals: agate, beryl, bloodstone, diamond, garnet (except sexual strength).

Associated Base Oil: none.

Purification

Associated Plants: acacia, anise, bay, benzoin, broom, calamus, camphor, chamomile, cedar, cinnamon, clove, copal, dill, eucalyptus, fennel, frankincense, garlic, ginger, gum arabic, hyssop, jasmine, juniper, lavender, lemon, lemon balm, lemongrass, lemon verbena, lilac, lime, myrrh, olive, orange, peppermint, pine, rosemary, sandalwood, thyme, tulip, valerian, vervain.

Associated Extracts and Concentrations: anise (tincture), bay (oil), benzoin (tincture or oil), bergamot (oil), camphor (oil), chamomile (oil), cedar wood (oil), cinnamon (oil), clove (oil), copal (tincture), eucalyptus (oil), fennel seed (oil), frankincense (oil), ginger (oil), gum arabic (tincture), jasmine (absolute), juniper berry (oil), lavender (oil), lemon (oil), lemongrass (oil), lime (oil), musk* (oil), myrrh (oil), neroli (oil) orange (oil), peppermint (oil), pine (oil), rosemary (oil), sandalwood (oil), thyme (oil).

Associated Minerals: aquamarine, calcite, salt (sea).

Associated Base Oil: olive.

Sexual Energy in Men, to stimulate a sense of

Associated Plants: allspice, banana, beans, carnation, dragon's blood, oak, olive, palm (dates), rosemary, vanilla.

Associated Extracts and Concentrations: allspice berry (oil), dragon's blood (perfume oil), rosemary (oil), vanilla (tincture).

Associated Minerals: carnelian, sunstone.

Associated Base Oil: olive oil, palm oil.

Sexual Honesty/Purity, to maintain one's promise (whatever it may be)

Associated Plants: camphor, coconut, cucumber, hawthorn, lavender, pineapple, vervain, witch hazel.

Associated Extracts and Concentrations: camphor (oil), lavender (oil).

Associated Minerals: garnet (especially when worn with gold).

Associated Base Oil: coconut oil.

Note: Camphor, lavender, and marjoram are also listed under celibacy. Use only if celibacy is also part of your intent.

Sleep, to encourage

Associated Plants: celery, chamomile, cinquefoil, elder, hops, hyacinth, jasmine, lavender, lettuce, marjoram, passion flower, peppermint, rosemary, thyme, valerian, vervain.

Associated Extracts and Concentrations: bergamot (oil), chamomile (oil), jasmine (absolute), lavender (oil), peppermint (oil), rosemary (oil).

Associated Minerals: moonstone, peridot, tourmaline (blue).

Associated Base Oil: none.

Strength (physical), to encourage a sense of

Associated Plants: bay, carnation, mugwort, mulberry, pennyroyal, saffron, St. John's Wort, tea, thistle.

Associated Extracts and Concentrations: *bay (oil).*

Associated Minerals: agate, beryl, bloodstone, diamond, garnet.

Associated Base Oil: none.

Success at Trade/Business

Associated Plants: basil, benzoin, cinnamon, clove, patchouli.

Associated Extracts and Concentrations: basil (oil), benzoin (tincture or oil), cinnamon (oil), clove (oil), patchouli (oil).

Associated Minerals: anazonite, bloodstone, chrysoprase, malachite, tourmaline (green).

Associated Minerals specific to sales/persuasiveness: carnelian, celestine, sardonyx.

Success, to bring a positive outlook to promote

Associated Plants: cinnamon, clover, ginger, high john, lemon balm, rowan.

Associated Extracts and Concentrations: cinnamon (oil), ginger (oil), high john (tincture).

Associated Minerals: alexandrite, apache tear, aventurine, chalcedony, chrysoprase, jet, lepidolite, olivine, opal, sardonyx, tiger's-eye, turquoise (when given as a gift).

Associated Base Oil: none.

Peace, to promote a feeling of

Associated Plants: apple, broom, chamomile, catnip, gardenia, ginger, jasmine, lavender, lemon balm, lily, lily of the valley, marjoram, rose.

Associated Extracts and Concentrations: bergamot (oil), chamomile (oil), ginger (oil), jasmine (absolute), lavender (oil), rose (oil), ylang-ylang (absolute).

Associated Minerals: amethyst, aquamarine, aventurine, calcite, carnelian, chalcedony, chrysocolla, diamond, kunzite, lepidolite malachite, obsidian, rhodocrosite, rhodonite, sappire, sardonyx, sodalite, tourmaline (blue).

Associated Base Oil: none.

Prosperity, to promote a prosperous image of self

Associated Plants: almond, bayberry, bergamot, honeysuckle, mint, patchouli, pine, vervain.

Associated Extracts and Concentrations: bergamot (oil), patchouli (oil), pine (oil).

Associated Minerals: aventurine, bloodstone, calcite, chrysoprase, emerald, jade, olivine, opal, pearl, peridot, ruby, salt, sapphire, spinel, staurolite, tiger's eye, topaz, tourmaline (green).

Associated Base Oil: almond oil.

Prosperity, to assist in finding employment or advancement

Associated Plants: lucky hand root, patchouli, pecan.

Associated Extracts and Concentrations: patchouli (oil).

Associated Minerals: aventurine, bloodstone, calcite, cat's eye, chryso-prase, emerald, jade, olivine, opal, peridot, ruby, sapphire, spinel, staurolite, tiger's eye, topaz, tourmaline (green).

Associated Base Oil: almond.

Wisdom, to encourage contemplation of issues before action

Associated Plants: gum arabic, frankincense, iris, peach, sage, sandal-wood, sunflower.

Associated Extracts and Concentrations: gum arabic (tincture), frank-incense (oil), sage (oil) sandalwood (oil).

Associated Minerals: chrysocolla, jade, sodalite, sugalite.

Associated Base Oil: sunflower.

Wishes, to encourage connectivity between aspiration and action

Associated Plants: buckthorn, dandelion, hazel, job's tears, pomegran-ate, sage, sandalwood, sunflower, tonka, violet, walnut.

Associated Extracts and Concentrations: sage (oil), sandalwood (oil).

Associated Minerals: alexandrite, apache tear, aventurine, chalcedony, chrysoprase, jet, tiger's eye.

Associated Base Oil: none.

A Final Word

We walked in the main ritual of the Real Witches Ball 2000 with an American flag held high. With that flag, we cast a circle of protection because it is that flag that protects our religious freedom. During that ritual, the non-pagan husband of a very close friend saw that the flag had hit the ground. At the time, I did not notice that the plastic fitting that held the topmost corner of the flag had broken. Thinking the flag had hit the ground deliberately, he demanded the flag be surrendered because we did not know how to use it. He stormed off with the flag, intent on protecting it from further disgrace.

Sir, I salute you! Although your act of bravery was founded on our misunderstanding and a couple of drinks, you ran head on into the center of a riled-up mob of several hundred people when you saw something you felt was wrong. You willingly offered what could have easily been your life to protect the honor and dignity of your country. Although your wife tells me that you do not consider yourself pagan, I would like to think that your actions were the most pagan thing I saw at that year's event.

I refused to end that circle without the return of both the flag and the patriot who attempted to protect it. With their return, I apologized for my negligence. An honor guard was formed from current and former military personnel from the circle, and the flag was retired with an ongoing salute from almost everyone in the circle. That flag was later delivered to a local American Legion, where it was properly burnt and buried with respect, honor, and love, as is the custom of our military.

The event brings up an interesting question. Are the symbols of our freedom so sacred that we should put them away where they will be protected, or are they more useful when we take them out of their vaults for active use? In the case of a flag, we are confronted with the question of whether they should sit atop a 50-foot flagpole or be held in our arms. The answer is both.

At home and over our capitals, the flag should be honored with utter protection. But on the field of battle, those who fight for it should embrace it. There is an ancient custom of entering a battle with the flag bearer at the very front of the charge. Behind him is a line of other men waiting to pick up that sacred symbol should the original bearer fall. It was important because it symbolized what the rest of the combatants fought for. If by chance the first flag bearer was struck, he would toss the Stars and Stripes over his shoulder before hitting the ground. The next flag bearer would catch it with ease because he had absolutely no other focus. Even on the field of combat, his only intent was to insure that the flag continued to lead the charge. Man after man could falter under fire, but the flag was not allowed to fall because it was the embodiment of everything those men fought to protect.

When we are attempting to cause change, we are in a battle with the forces that resist that change. When such a battle involves issues of religious freedom, there is no better symbolism than the flag of a nation brave enough to guarantee that freedom. For that reason, I declare that if you live in one of these great nations, you should never enter unto that field of battle without your nation's flag as the very embodiment of that freedom. Hold it high at each of the Quarters and end that rite screaming the words, "We are free! Blessed Be!" over and over until you can scream no more.

I will continue the Real Witches Ball each October until I have no more breath to utter those words. At that point, I will insure that the legacy of what it has become lives on in another person's breath. Each year, we shall gather and discuss the demons that we have destroyed over the previous year. Each year, we will share information on how we managed to defeat those demons and identify areas where we need to improve our vigilance. Ongoing battles will be identified and what force we raise will be distributed to the areas that need reinforcement.

I do not know why this event has grown as it has and I do not know why it has taken the turns that it has. But it looks to be our best bet for social reform, so I beg of you to attend and feel the strength of our number. With that feeling, you will identify the truth that I arrived at this year; there is absolutely nothing we cannot change if that change is just!

Contact us at:

The Real Witches Ball Planning Committee
1209 North High Street
Columbus, Ohio USA 43201
Phone: (614) 421-7557
Web: *www.neopagan.com*
E-mail: mailbox@www.neopagan.com

Appendix A

Contact Information for Organizations

Special thanks to Ellen Evert Hopman, Druid from the Order of the Whiteoak (Ord na Darach Gile), for assembling the great amount of this contact information. Additional thanks to Osyr and Celene, two close friends, for presenting it at the Real Witches Ball 2000.

The American Civil Liberty Union   Check local information
www.aclu.org

Note: The A.C.L.U. does not have one central phone number to make referrals to each area. It does have an image map of the United States on its Web site that offers local contacts, but failing connectivity to the Web site, you will have to call local information to secure a phone number.

American Foundation for Aids Research   212-806-1600
www.amfar.org

Beyond all other motivations, it wants to prevent HIV infection and eventually discover a cure.

Gay Men's Health Crisis   212-367-1536
www.gmhc.org

The oldest AIDS information organization in the United States. Counseling available.

Greenpeace   800-326-0959
www.greenpeace.org

Protection of marine wildlife and other natural habitats as well as anti-nuclear activism.

The Humane Society of the United States   800-808-7858
www.hsus.org

More than just the local pound. The Humane Society is the largest animal rights advocates in the United States.

Human Rights Campaign   800-777-hrcf
www.hrc.org

The largest gay and lesbian advocacy organization in the United States.

International Rescue Committee   800-551-3000
www.intrescom.org

Not-for-profit organization seeking protection and resettlement services for victims of oppression.

The National Wildlife Federation   800-822-9919
www.nwf.org

Main focus is on endangered and threatened animals and their habitats.

National Abortion Rights Action League   202-973-3000
www.naral.org

As an adopted child, I agree with my mother's view on abortion. It is not something we hope to ever have to choose, but taking that right to choose away from a potential parent is not the act of a religion that encourages choice. NARAL is the political arm of the pro-choice movement.

Oxfam America   800-77o-xfam
www.oxfamamerica.org

Mother Nature is not always nice and these folk help those affected
by her temper. Emergency assistance for victims of hurricanes, floods,
and other natural disasters as well as refugees of war and war like
actions. Side note: My insurance company says I am not protected for
acts of war and notes that all nuclear detonations are considered acts
of war.

Seashepherd Society   No listed phone contact
www.seashepherd.org

Investigates and documents violations of international laws to protects marine wildlife.

U.N.I.C.E.F.   800-for-kids
www.unicefusa.org

The United Nations International Children's Emergency Fund was
founded to protect children and their mothers. Consider the nature
of our horned god and ask what better cause could a male Wiccan
support?

Appendix B

Spellcraft Sources

Think global, purchase local!

It is always best to handle, touch, and smell anything that you will use in spellcraft before you purchase it. Before resorting to any of these sources, please first refer to your local yellow pages. If you look up "herbs" you will probably find suppliers of both herbs and oils that are just around the corner.

What follows is a list of suppliers that come from the heart. They are not paid endorsements. As such, I would very much appreciate it if you told them you found their name and address in my book. It helps us to let the circle of family and friends know who has been thinking about them.

Azure Green
PO Box 48 WSFM
Middlefield, MA 01243-0048
(413) 623-2155
www.azuregreen.com

Azure Green (formerly Abyss Distribution) is a general retail & wholesale distributor. You can not find a better group of people to do business with.

Magickal Moments
12 Pine Street
Easthampton, MA 01027
(413) 529-0760

Great folk with a great product. Remember that even if you purchase a candle locally, it may have been made in China. Better to order your candles here or insist that your local store does the ordering. Their magickal oils are sold ready to use.

Nuit Unlimited Imports
12612 Oak Knoll Road
#7
Poway, CA 92064
858-486-8325

The single best Abramelin Oil in the world! Challenging the industry, Nuit Unlimited supplies magickal oils that contain only true essentials. Without base oils, they do tend to appear more pricey, but when you consider what it is that you are purchasing, these are probably some of the most reasonably priced magickal oils on the market today.

Salem West
1209 North High Street
Columbus, OH 43201
(614) 421-7557
www.neopagan.com

Owned by yours truly. We are one of the largest neopagan shops in the Midwest, but because we are a family owned and operated shop that focuses mostly on interactive sales, our print catalog is only available during times when we can handle the increase in business. Visit our Web site for our current electronic catalog.

Bibliography

Although unpublished works are not generally cited in bibliographies, it is necessary here to include the unpublished and untitled works and translations of Tatia Kingslady. Within the portions of that bulk of work, on which I drew heavily, specific passages were cited as follows:

Practical Instruction in Infantry Campaigning Exercise (1884) (French)

The Tarot: A Short Treatise on Reading Cards (French)

The Fall of Granada: A Poem in Six Duans (1885) (French)

Egyptian Symbolism (Published in Paris)

The Tarot, Its Occult Significance and Methods of Play (1888) (French)

Books

Crowley, Aleister. *777*. New York: Weiser, 1973.

Cunningham, Scott. *The Complete Book of Incense, Oils and Brews.* St Paul, MN: Llewellyn, 1989.

—. *Cunningham's Encyclopedia of Crystal, Gem and Metal Magic.* St. Paul, MN: Llewellyn, 1988.

—. *Cunningham's Encyclopedia of Magical Herbs.* St. Paul, MN: Llewellyn, 1985.

Drew, A.J. *Wicca for Men.* New York: Kensington, 2000.

Elias, Marilyn. "Power of Prayer Passes Muster in AIDS Study, Arlington, VA." *USA Today*, 12 March 1998, 1d.

Farrar, Janet and Stewart. *The Witches' God.* Washington: Phoenix, 1989.

Knight, Sirona. *Dream Magic.* San Francisco: Harper, 2000.

———. *Love, Sex, and Magick.* New York: Kensington 2000.

———. *Pocket Guide to Celtic Spirituality.* Freedom, CA: Crossing, 1998.

———. *Pocket Guide to Crystals and Gemstones.* Freedom, CA: Crossing, 1998.

Mathers, MacGregor. *Astral Projection Ritual Magic and Alchemy.* London: Neville Spearman, 1971.

Mathers, MacGregor (translator). *The Book of the Sacred Magic of Abramelin the Mage.* New York: Dover, 1975.

———. *The Grimoire of Armadel.* Maine: Weiser, 1994.

———. *The Key of Solomon the King.* Maine: Weiser, 1972.

———. *The Qabbalah Unveiled.* Arkana, 1992.

———. *The Tarot.* Maine: Weiser, 1993.

Morrison, Dorothy. *Everyday Magic.* St. Paul, MN: Llewellyn, 1998.

O'hara, Gwydion. *The Magick of Aromatherapy*. St. Paul, MN: Llewellyn, 1998.

Slate, Joe. *Aura Energy*. St. Paul, MN: Llewellyn, 1999.

Telesco, Patricia. *365 Goddess*. San Francisco: Harper, 1998.

———. *Advanced Wicca*. New York: Kensington, 2000.

———. *A Charmed Life*. Franklin Lakes, NJ: New Page, 2000.

———. *Dancing with Devas*. Laceyville, PA: Belfry Books, 1998.

———. *FutureTelling*. Freedom, CA: Crossing, 1998.

———. *Ghosts, Spirits and Hauntings*. Freedom, CA: Crossing, 1999.

———. *A Little Book of Love Magic*. Freedom, CA: Crossing, 1999.

———. *Goddess in My Pocket*. San Francisco: Harper, 1998.

———. *Mirror, Mirror: Reflections of the Sacred Self*. Sun Lakes, AZ: Blue Star, 1999.

———. *Seasons of the Sun*. Maine: Weiser, 1996.

———. *Shaman in a 9 to 5 World*. Freedom, CA: Crossing, 2000.

———. *Spinning Spells and Weaving Wonders*. Freedom, CA: Crossing, 1995.

———. *Wicca 2000*. New York: Kensington, 2000.

———. *The Wiccan Book of Ceremonies and Rituals*. New York: Kensington, 2000

——— *Wishing Well*. Freedom, CA: Crossing 1997.

Index

About the Author

A. J. Drew, the author of the groundbreaking book *Wicca for Men*, is the owner of Salem West, one of the largest neopagan/ Wiccan shops in the Midwest. A.J. also hosts The Real Witches Ball, one of the single largest pagan gatherings in the United States, and is the founder of *www.neopagan.com*, which was designed to be an online hub for the entire pagan community.